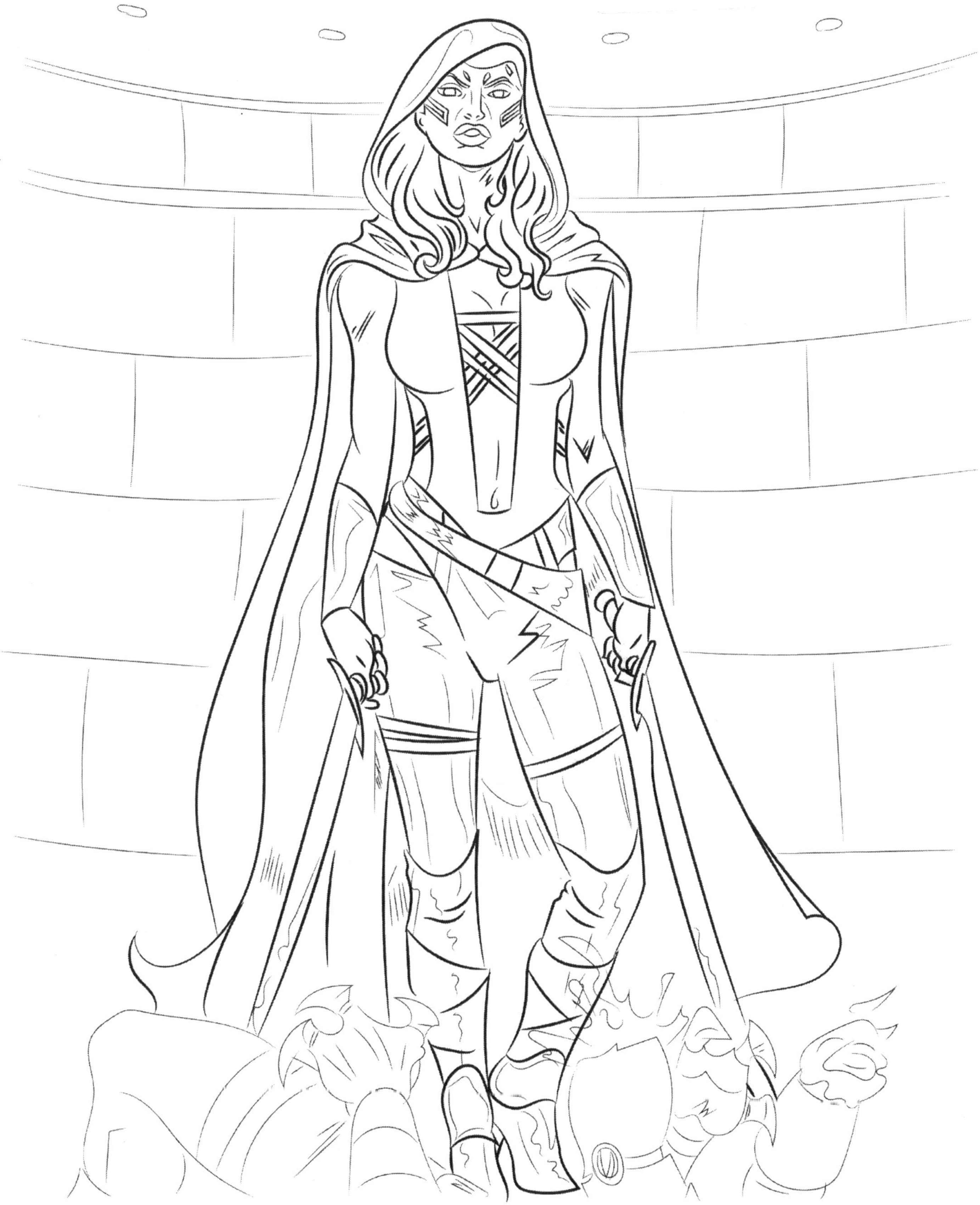

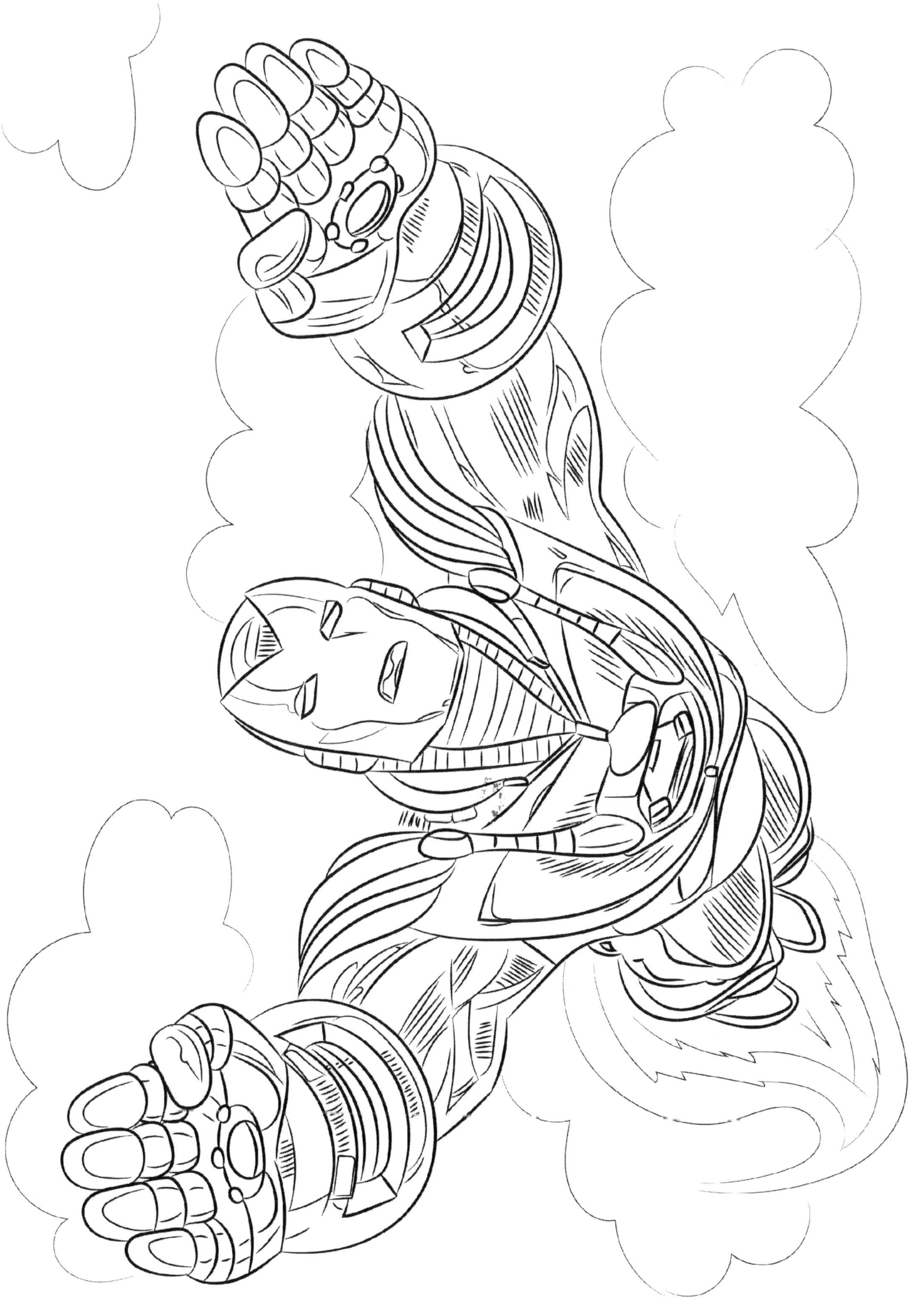

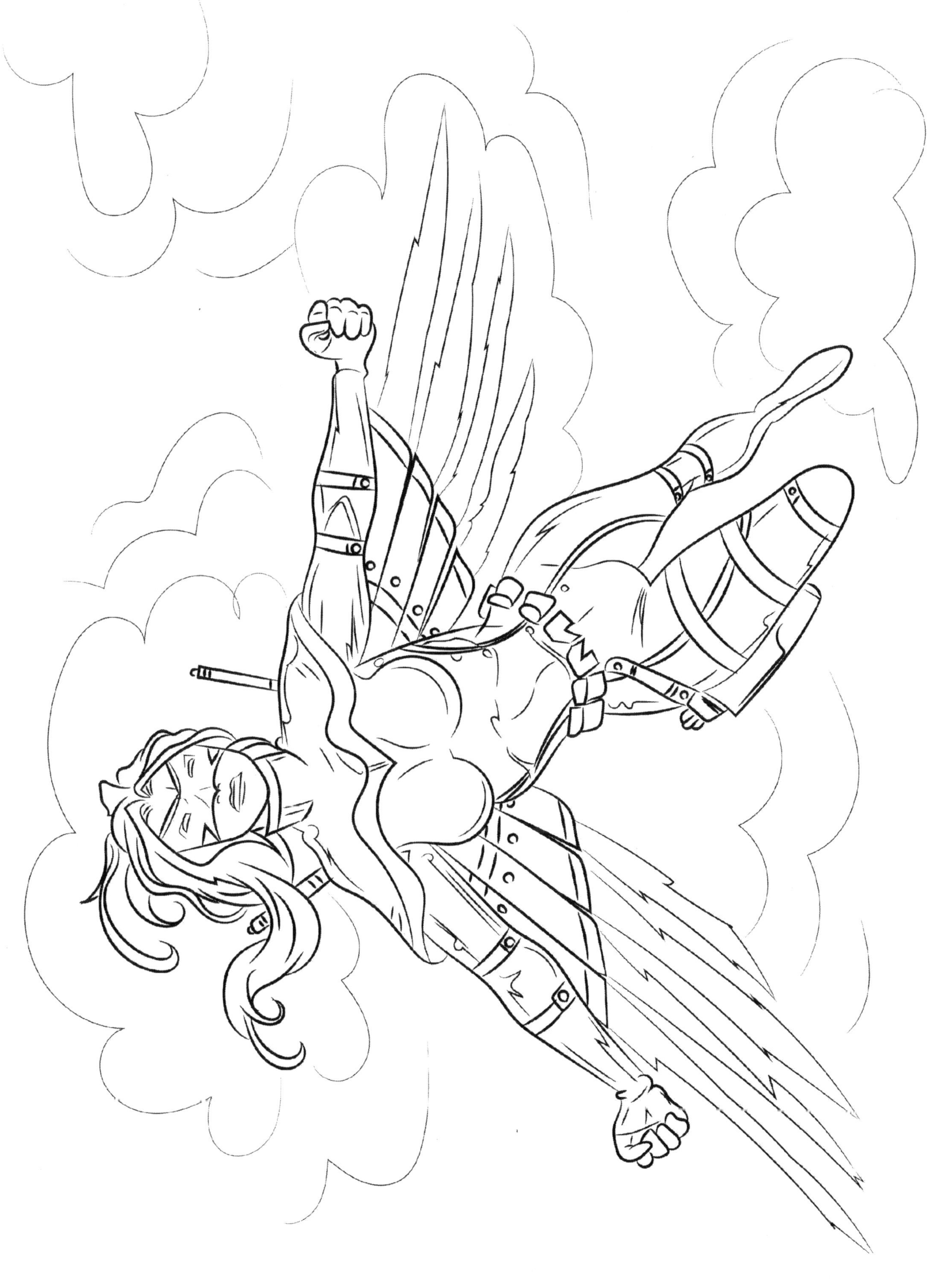

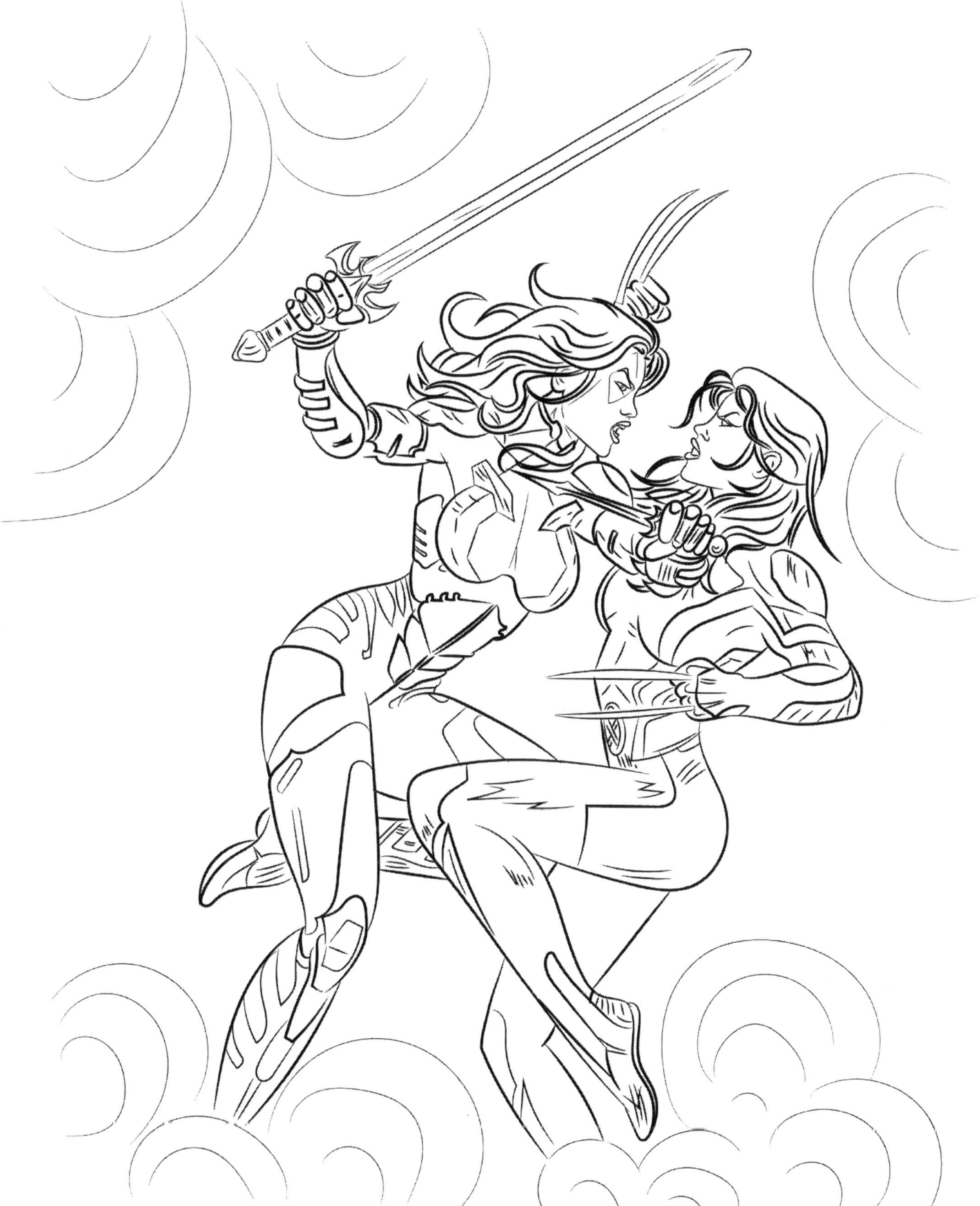

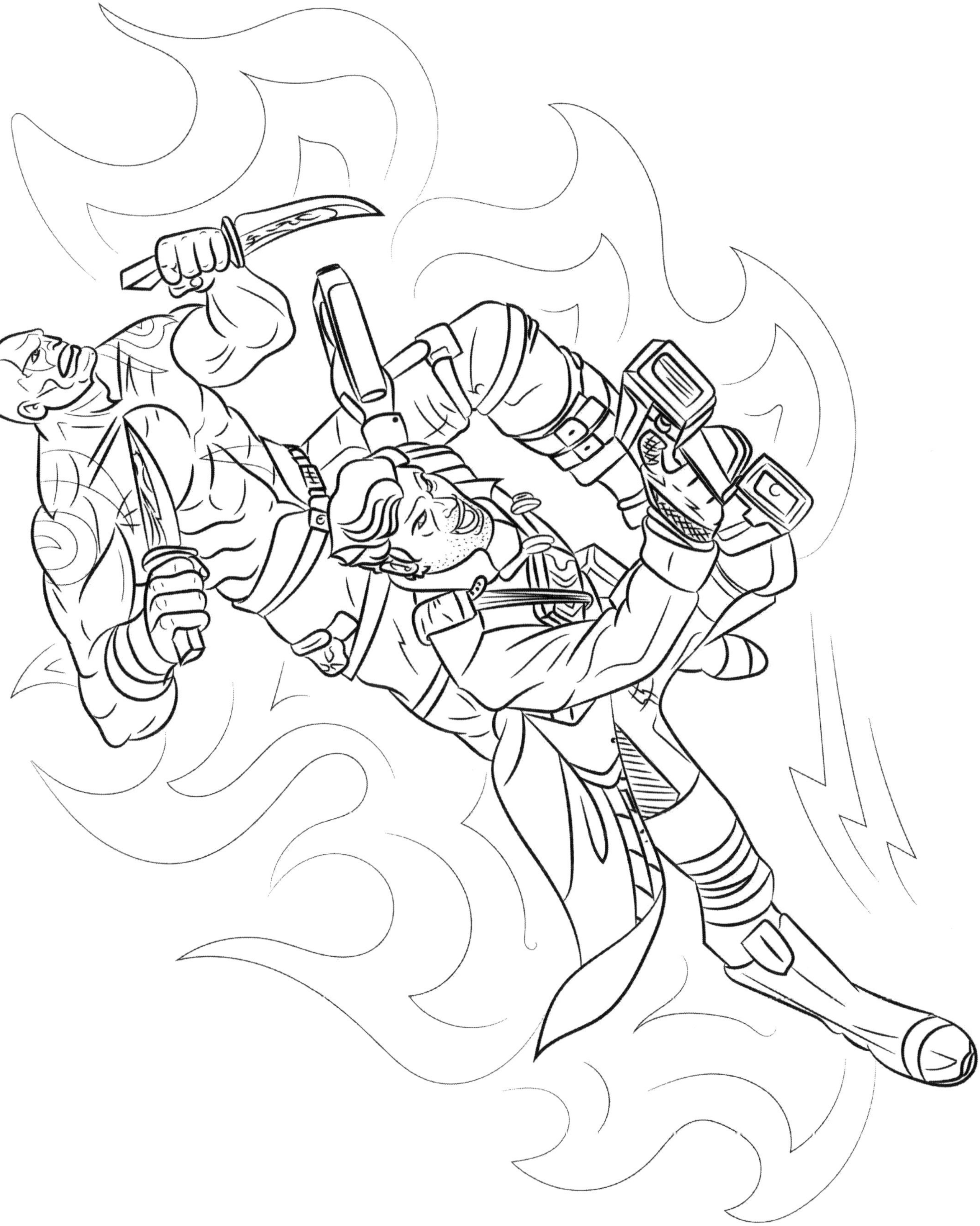

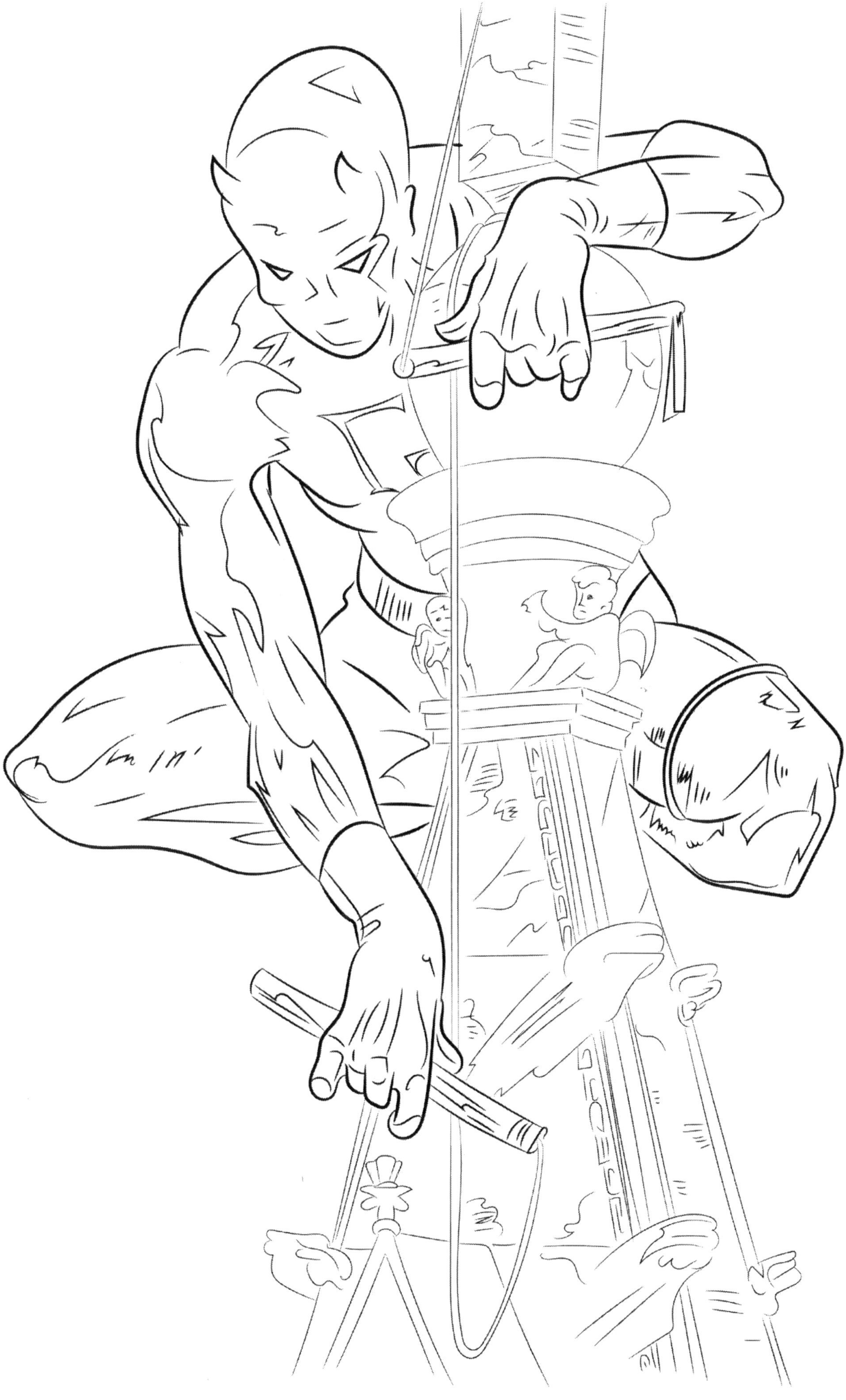

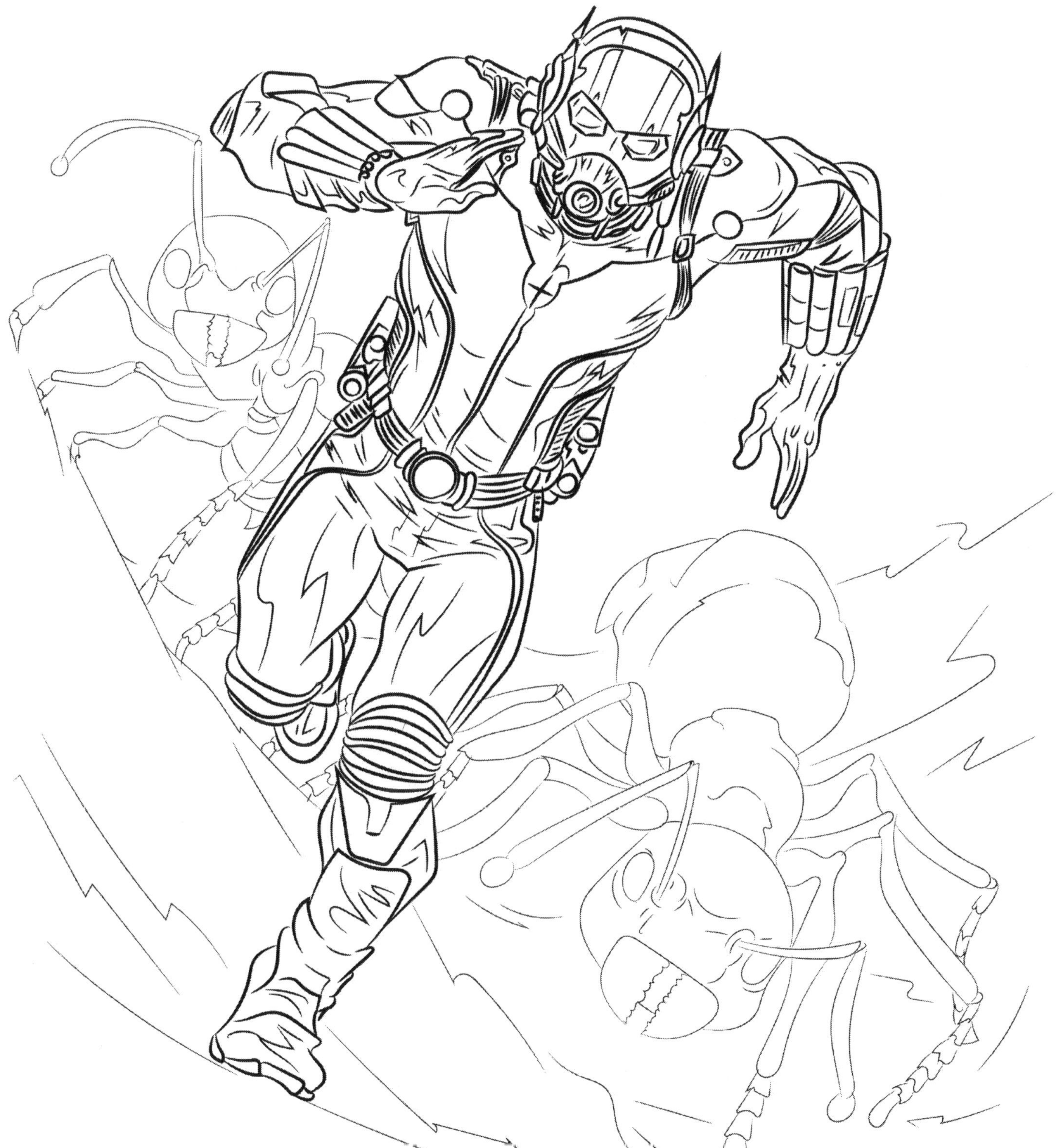

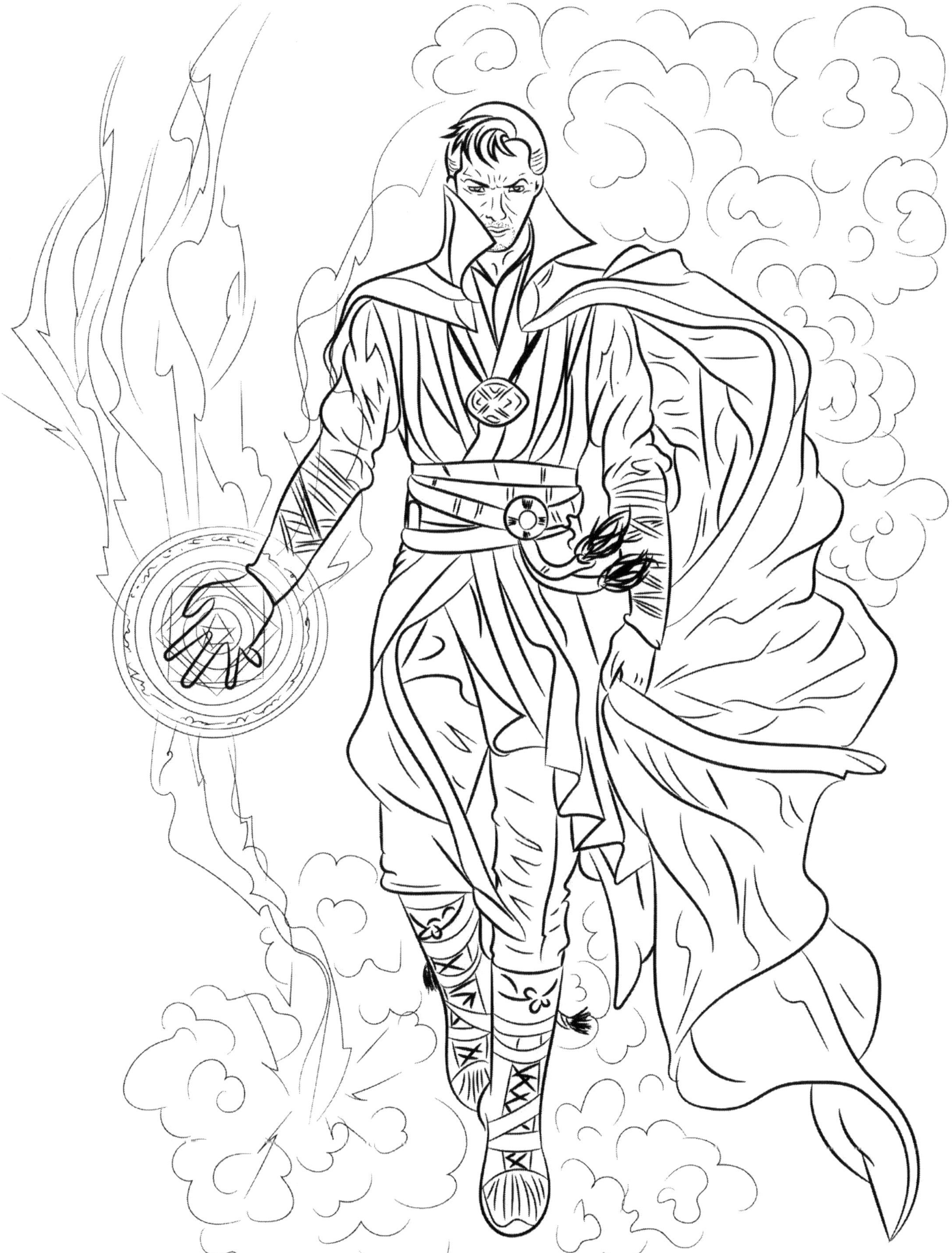

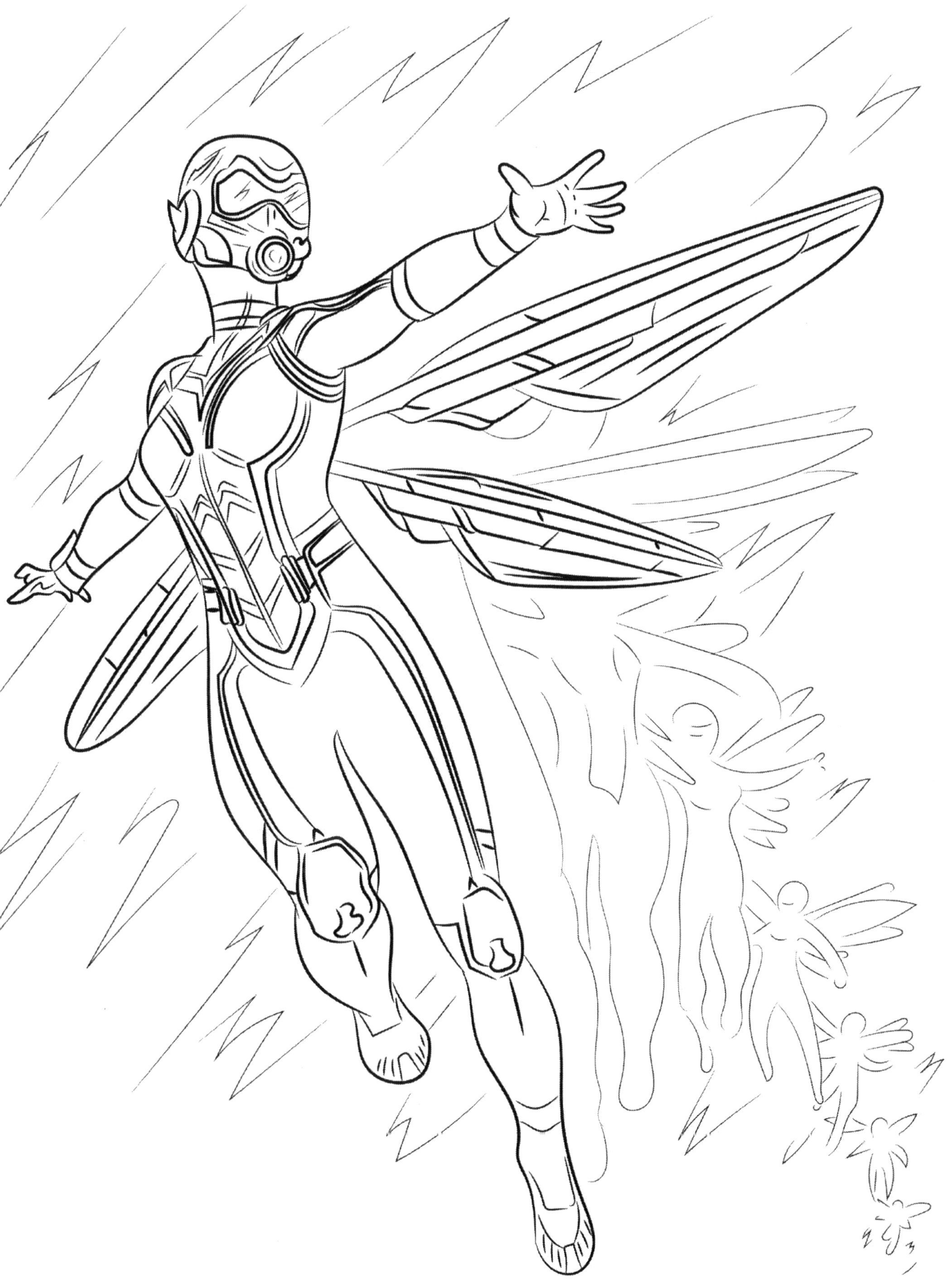

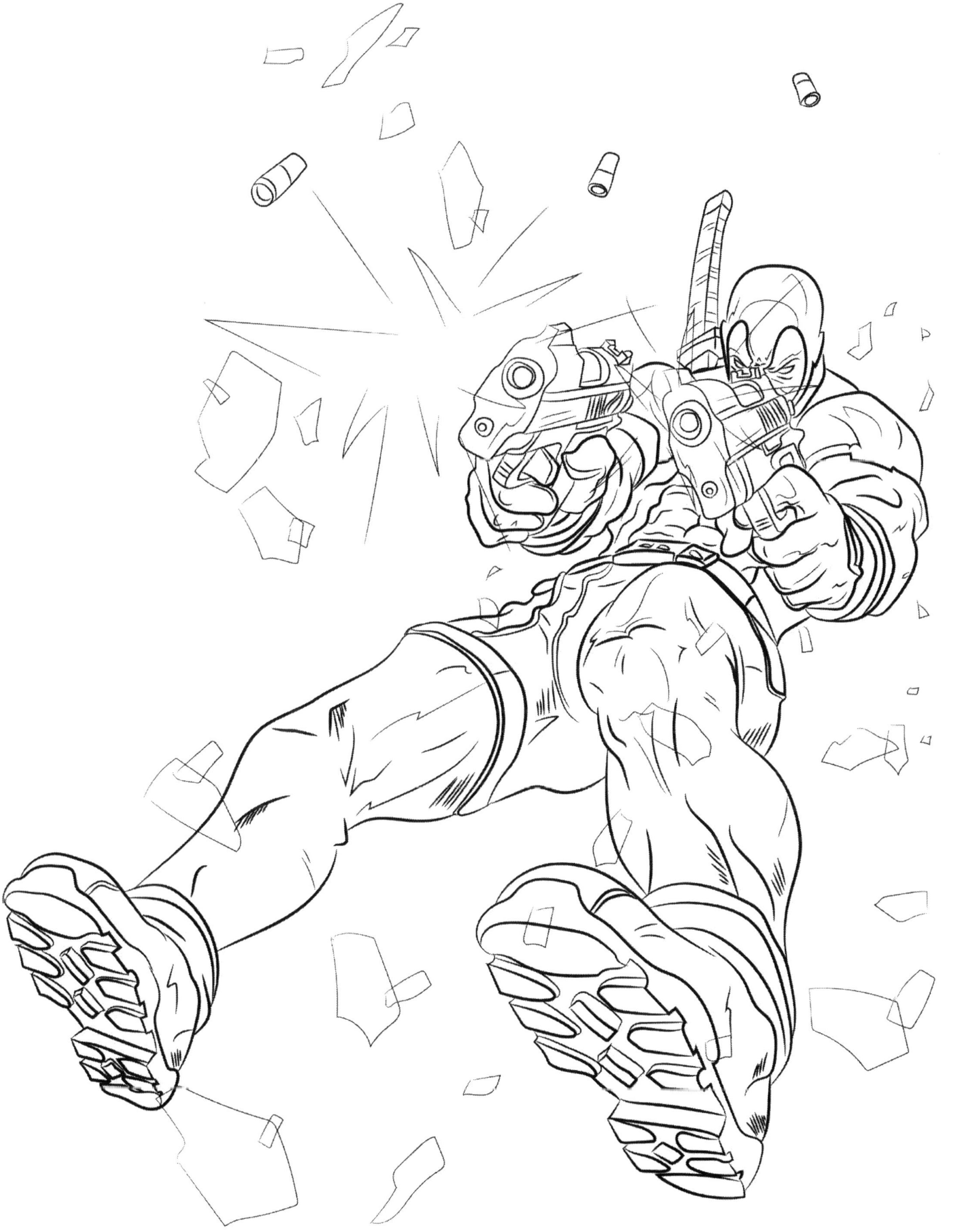

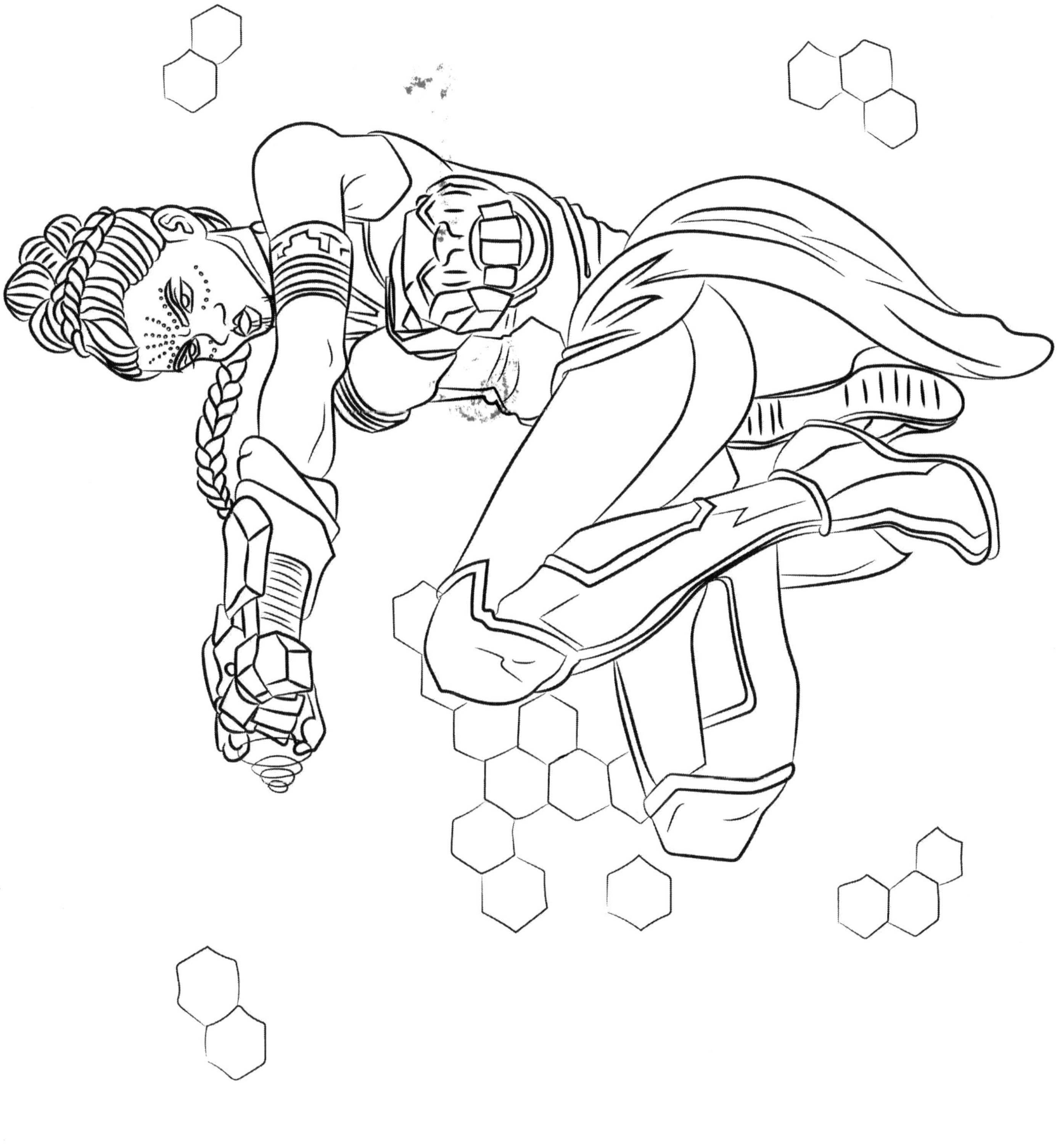

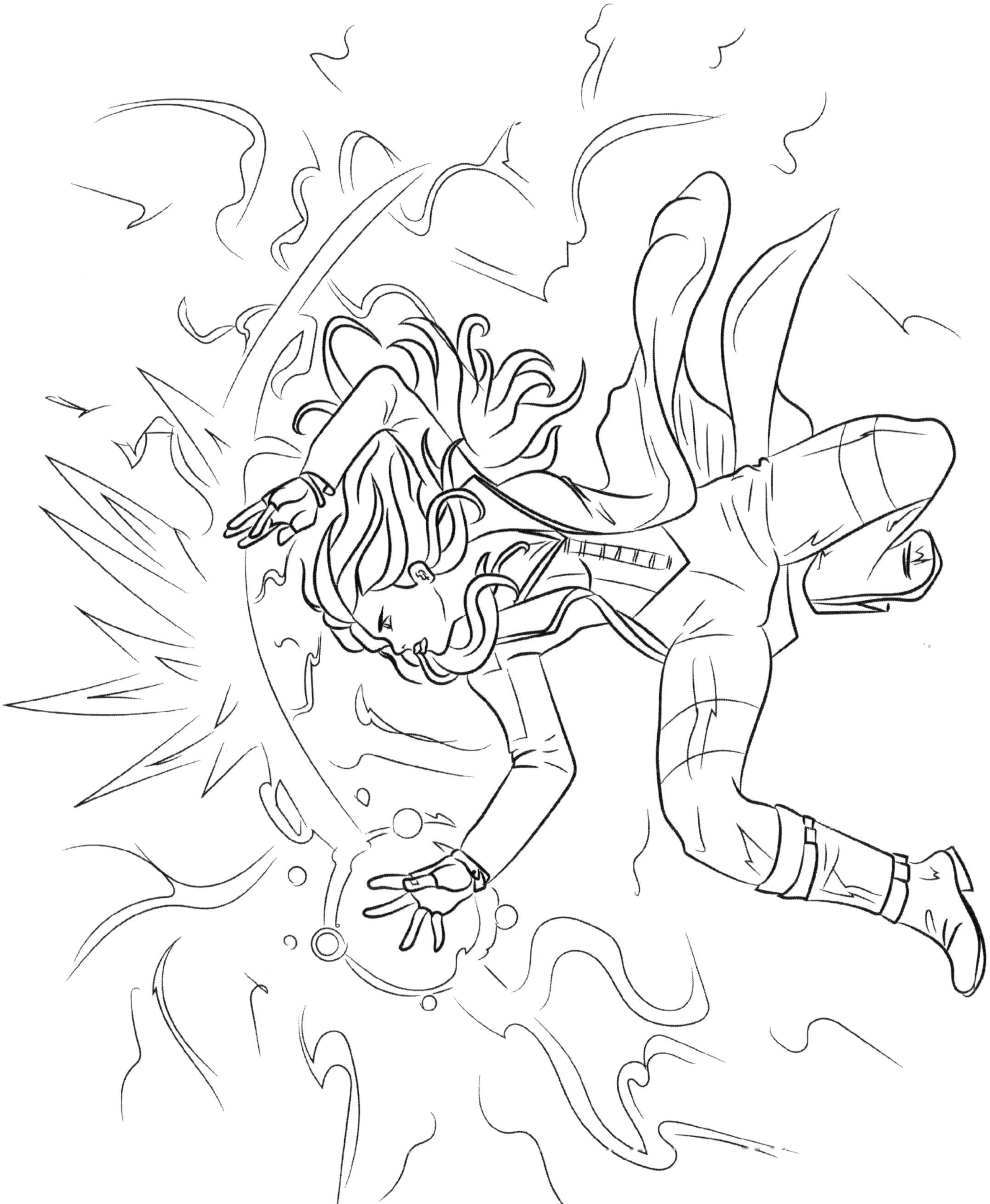

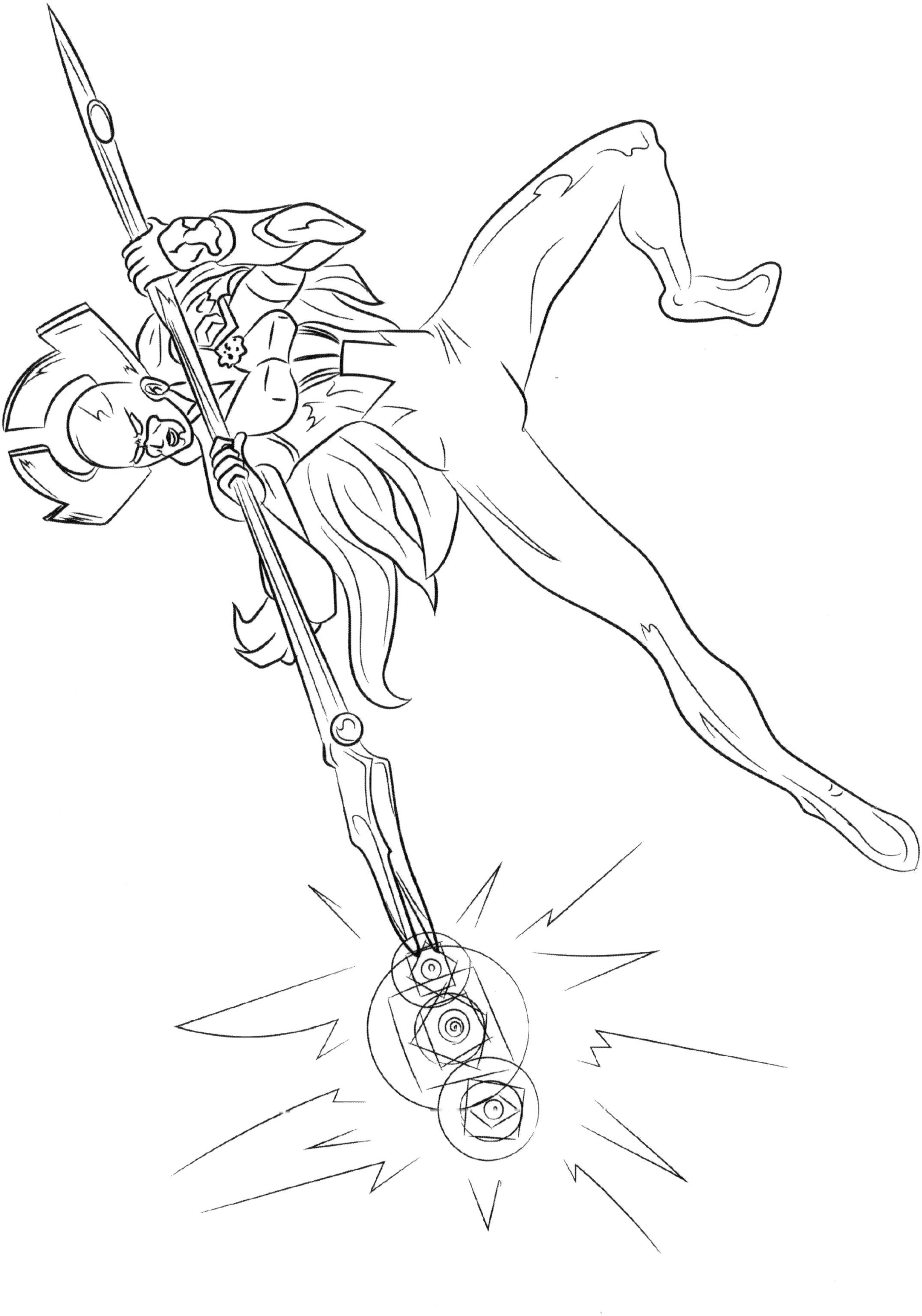

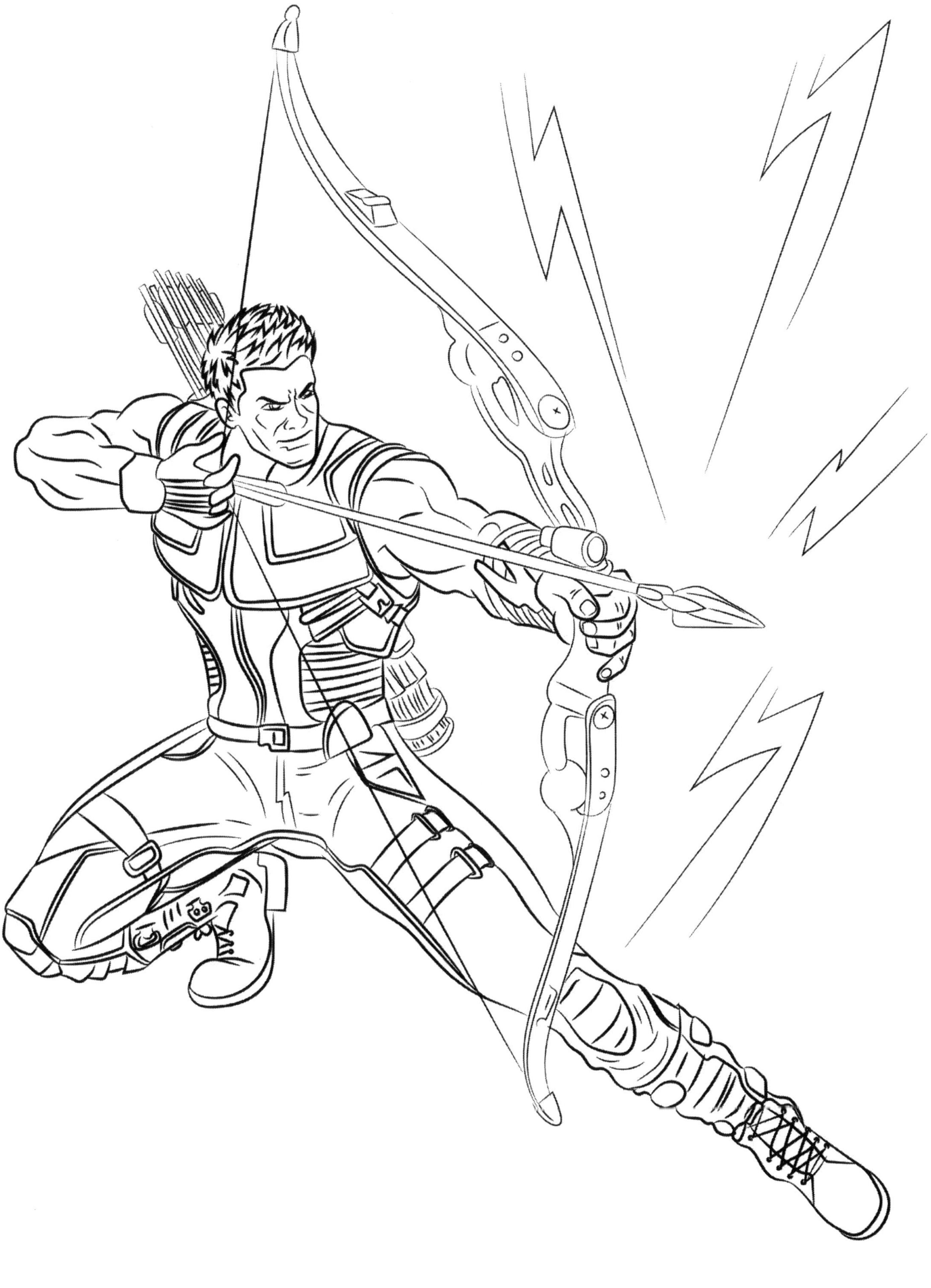

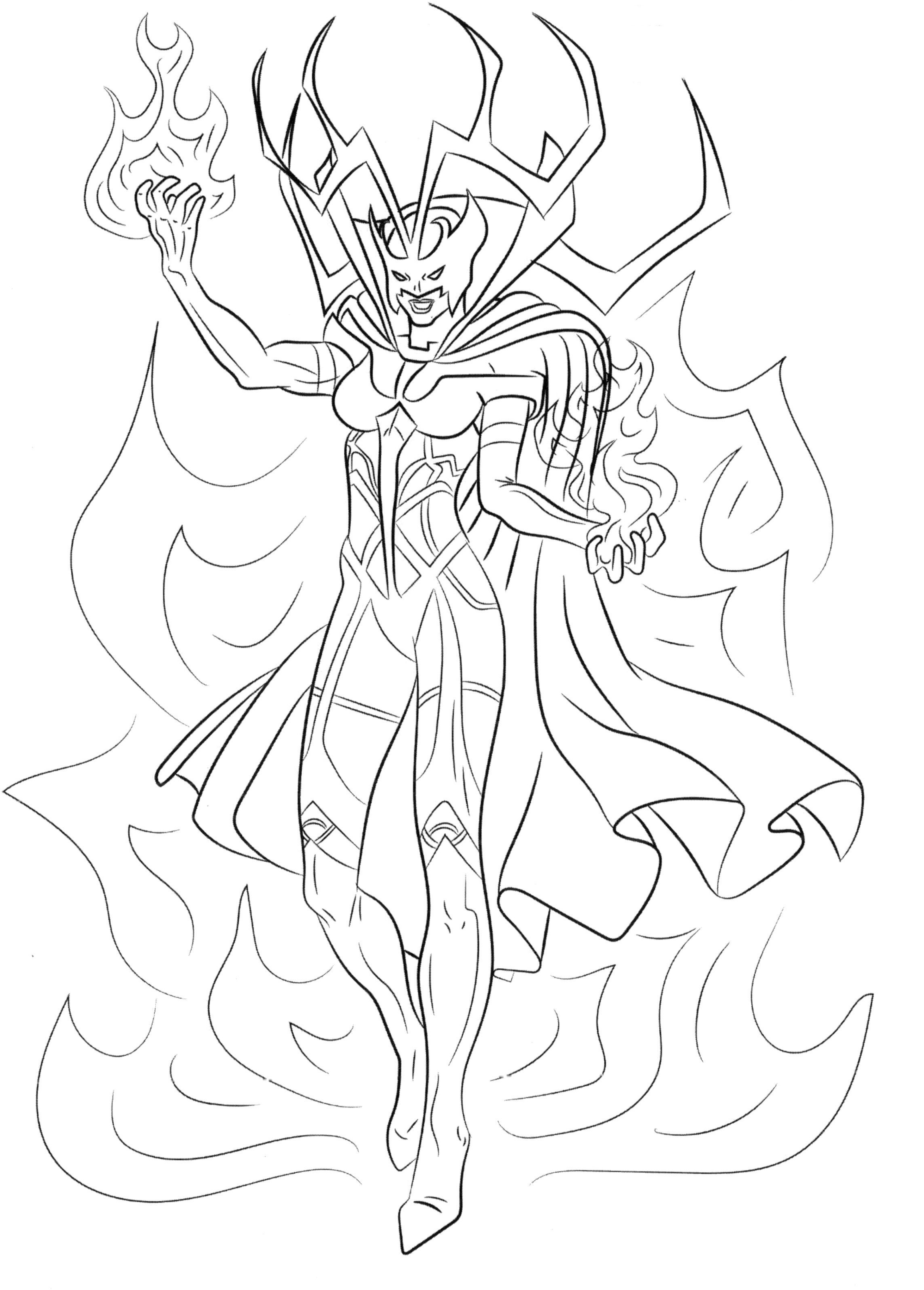

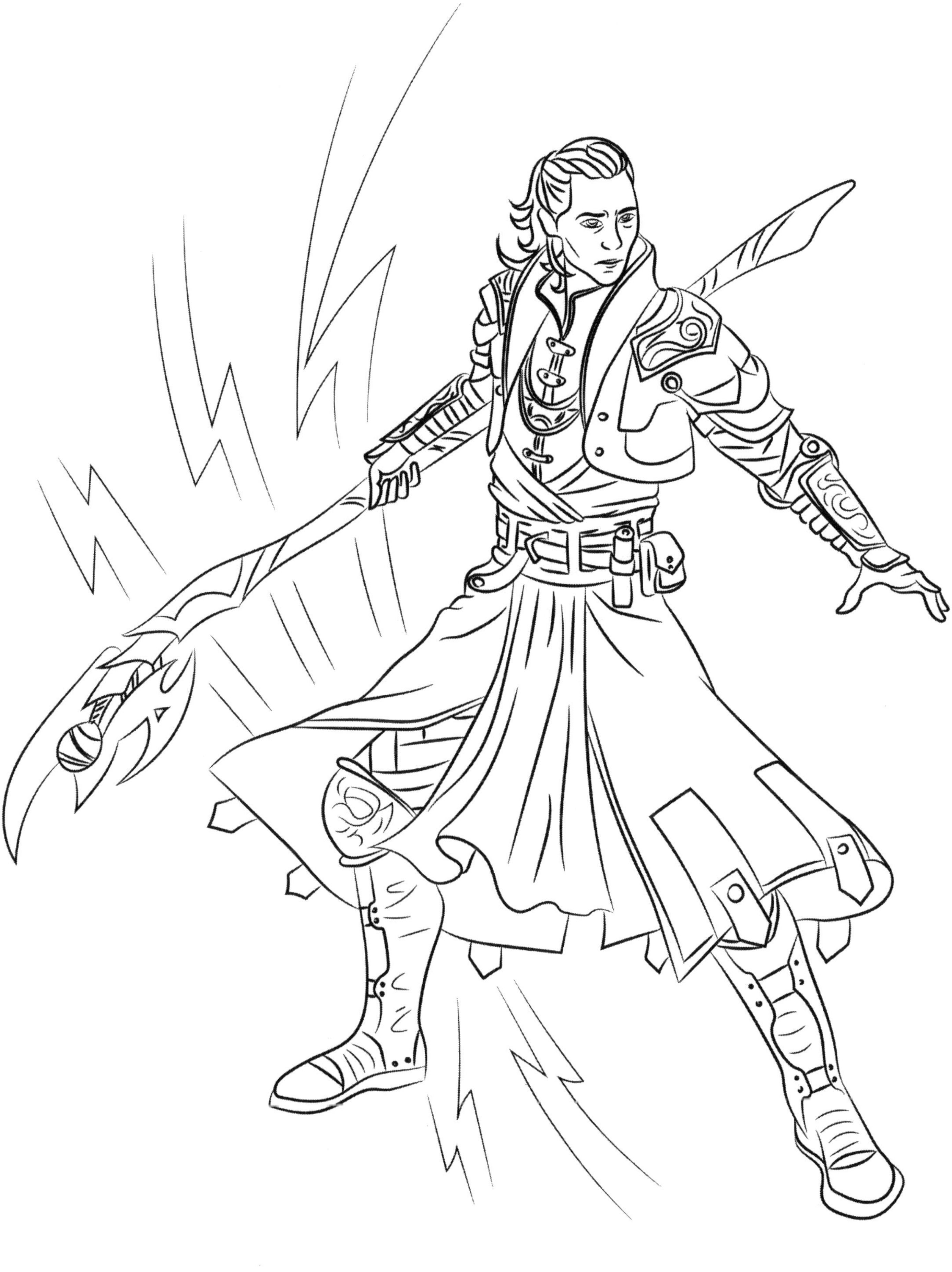

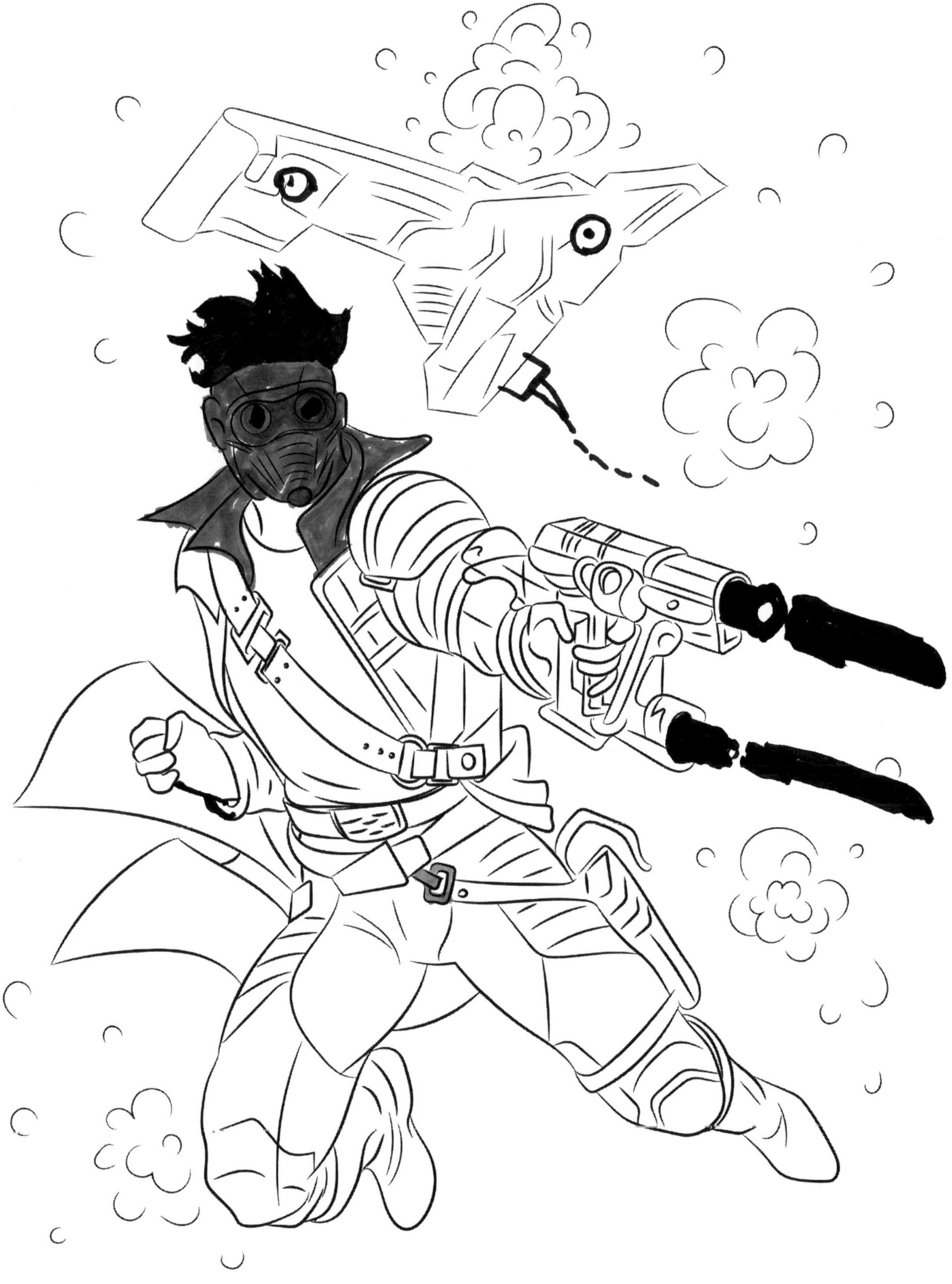

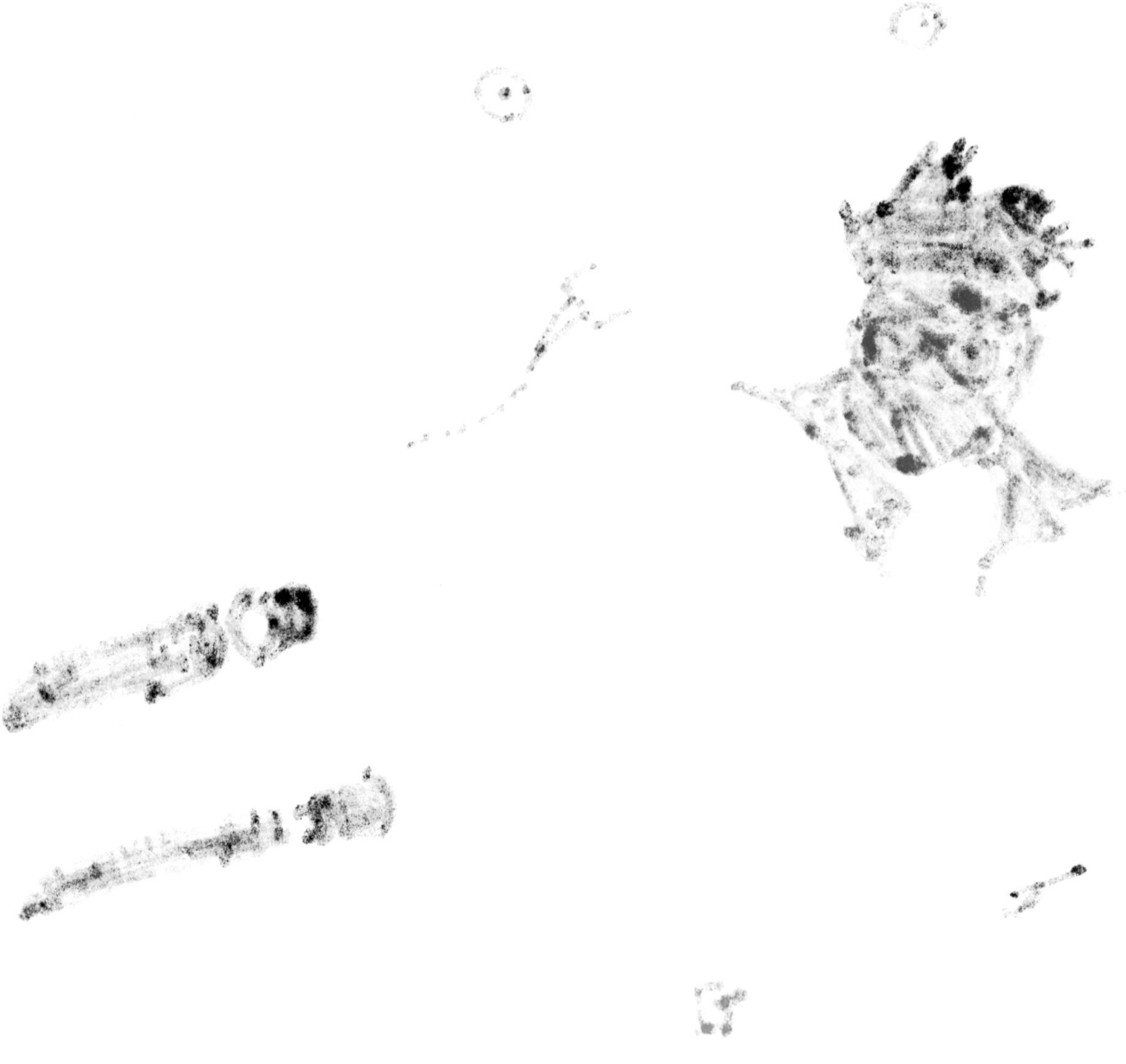

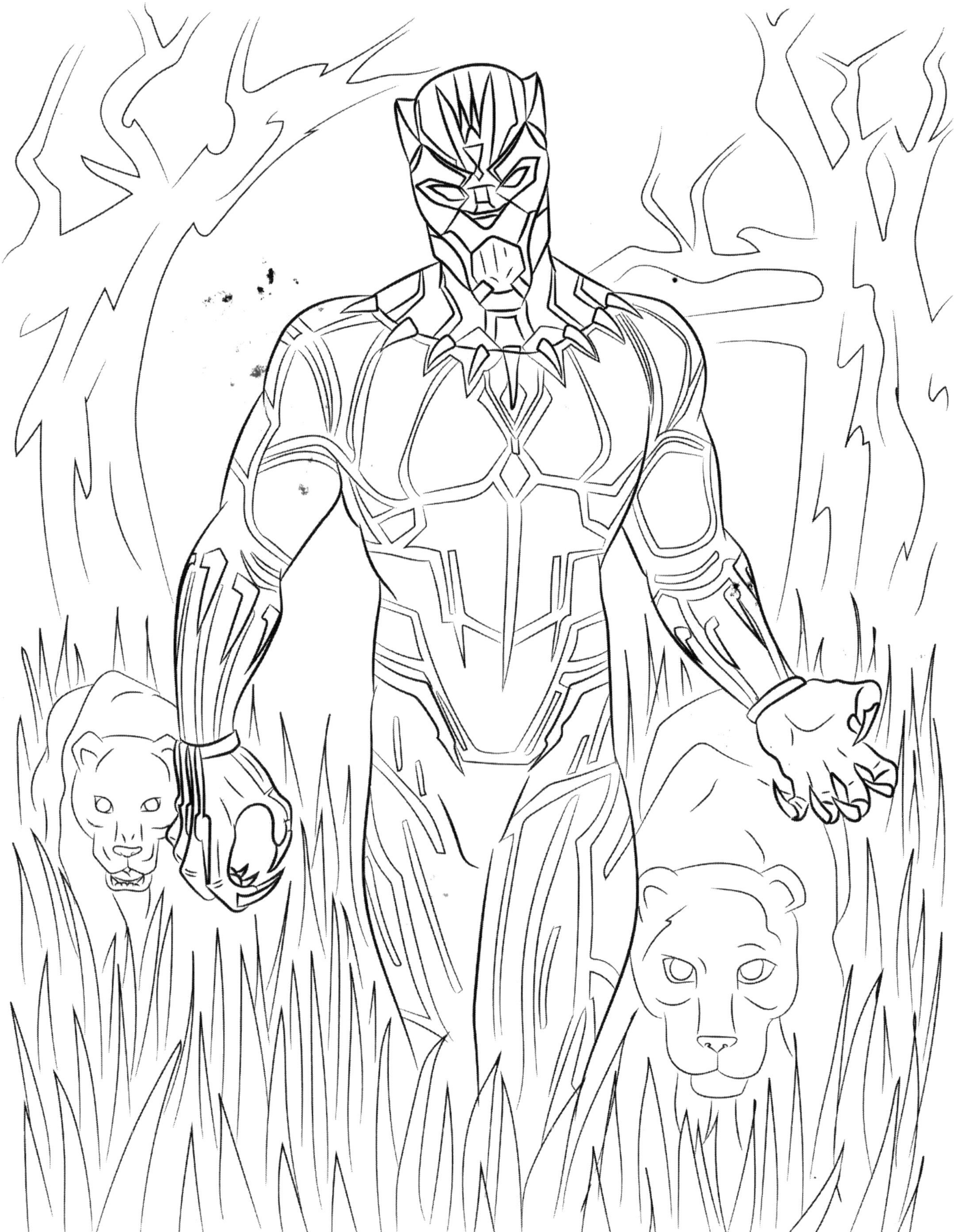

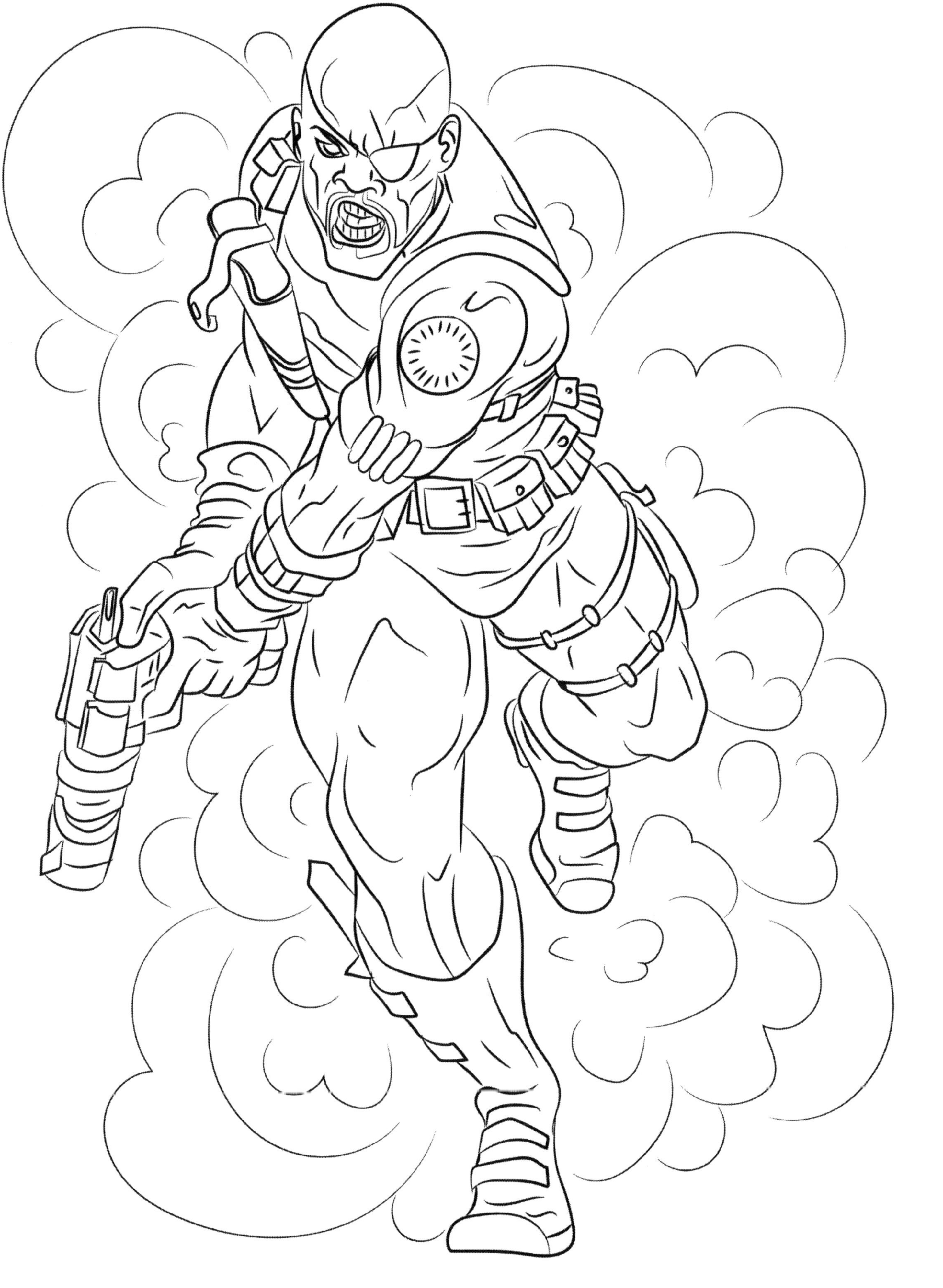

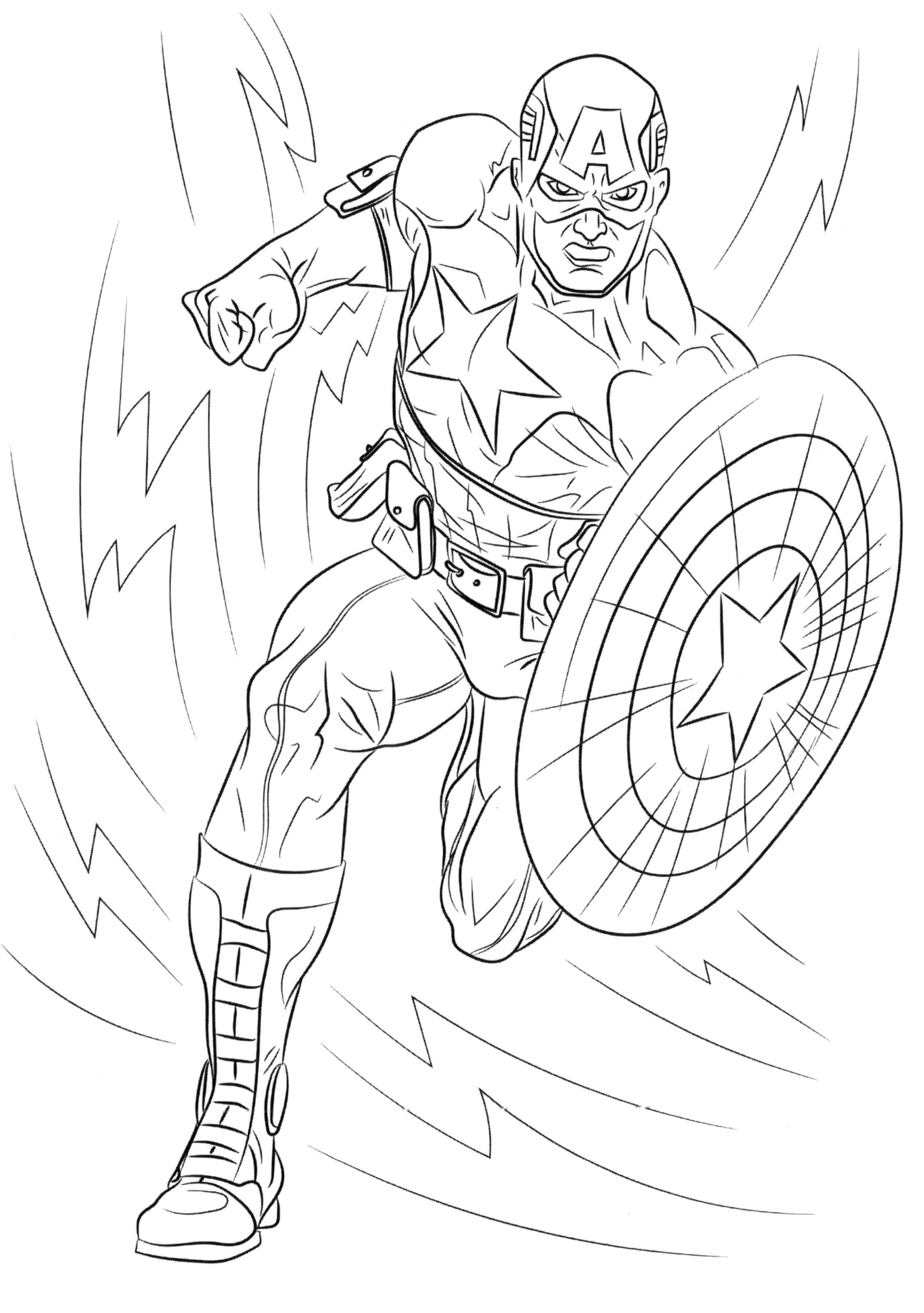

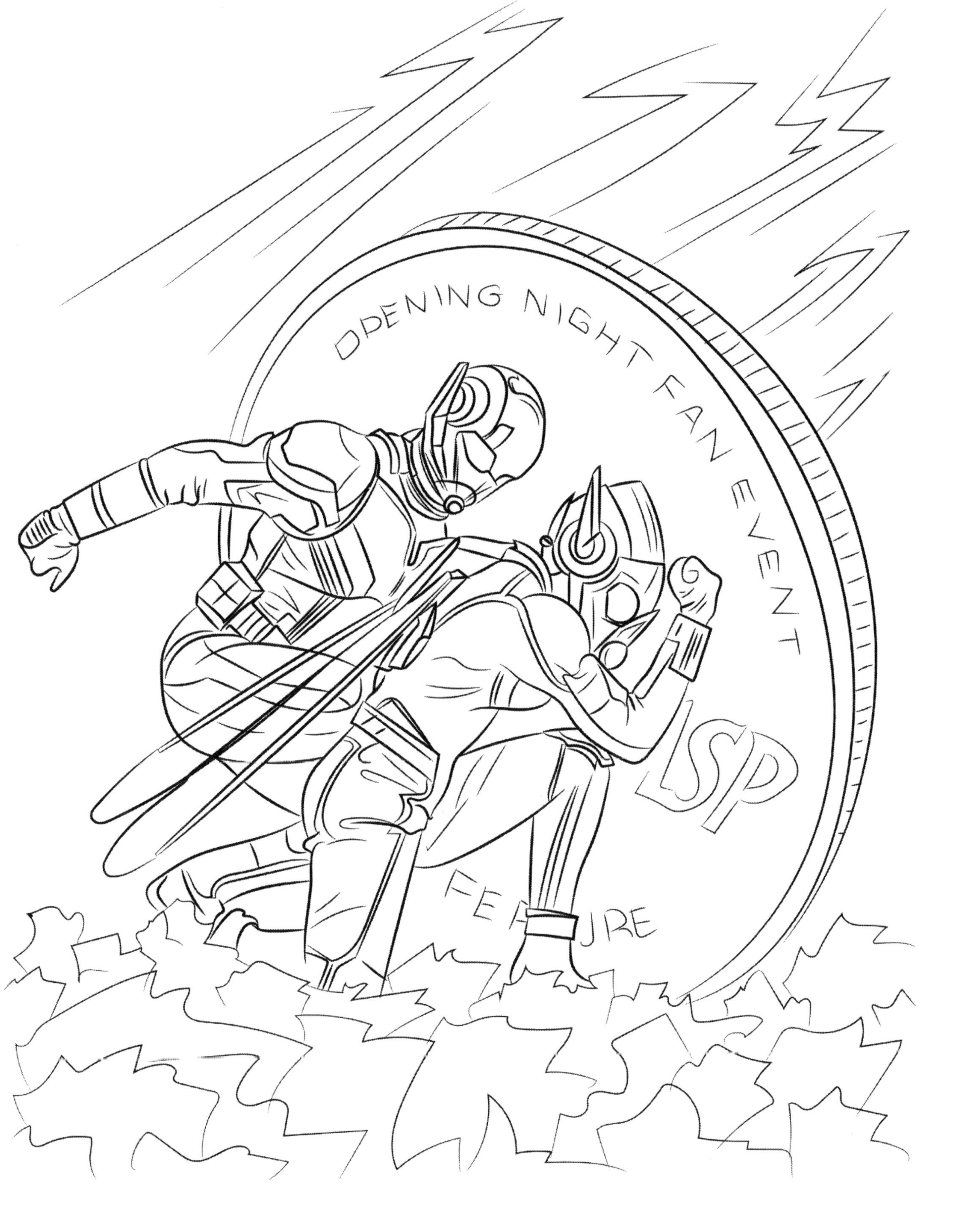
OPENING NIGHT FAN EVENT

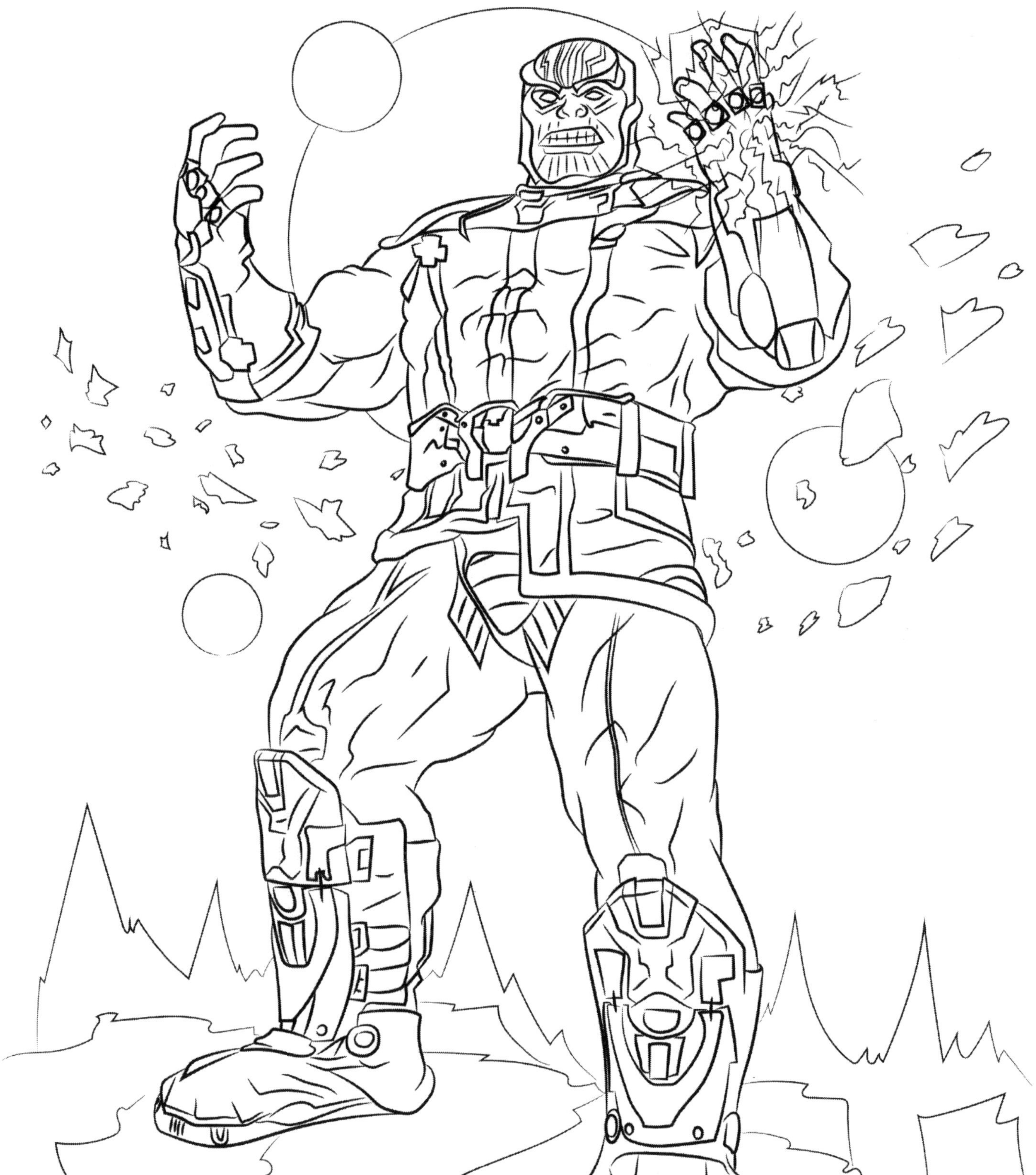

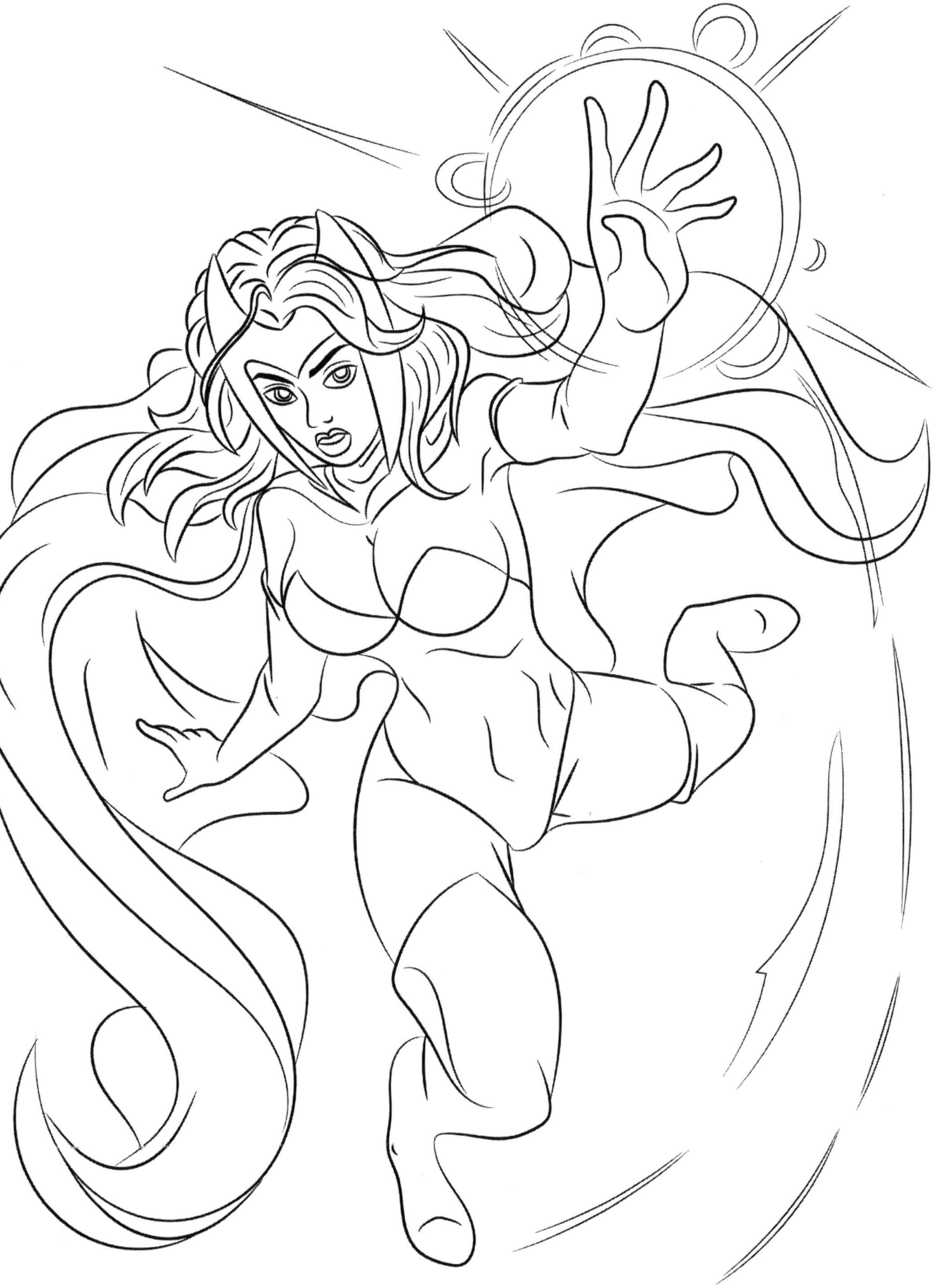

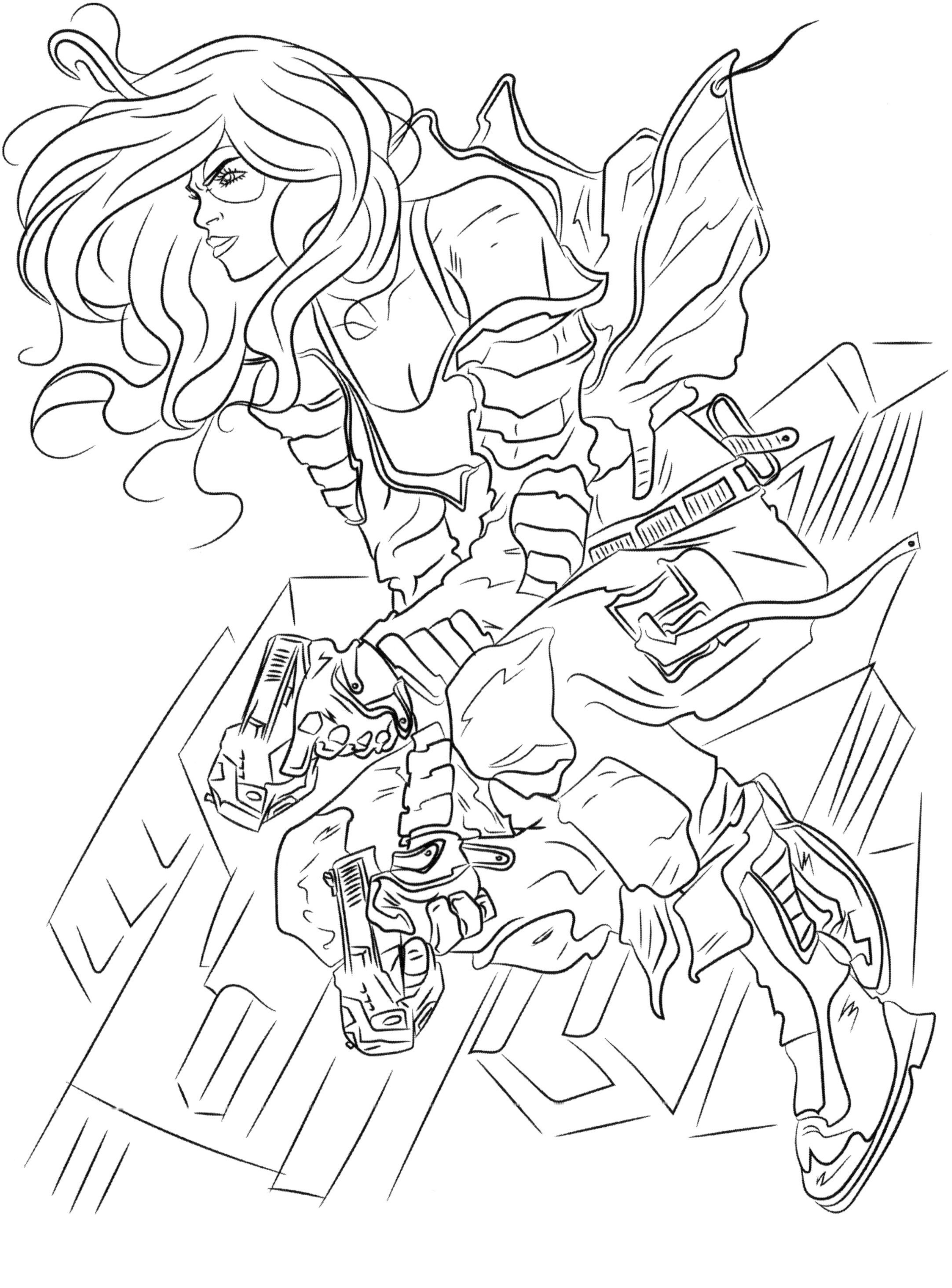

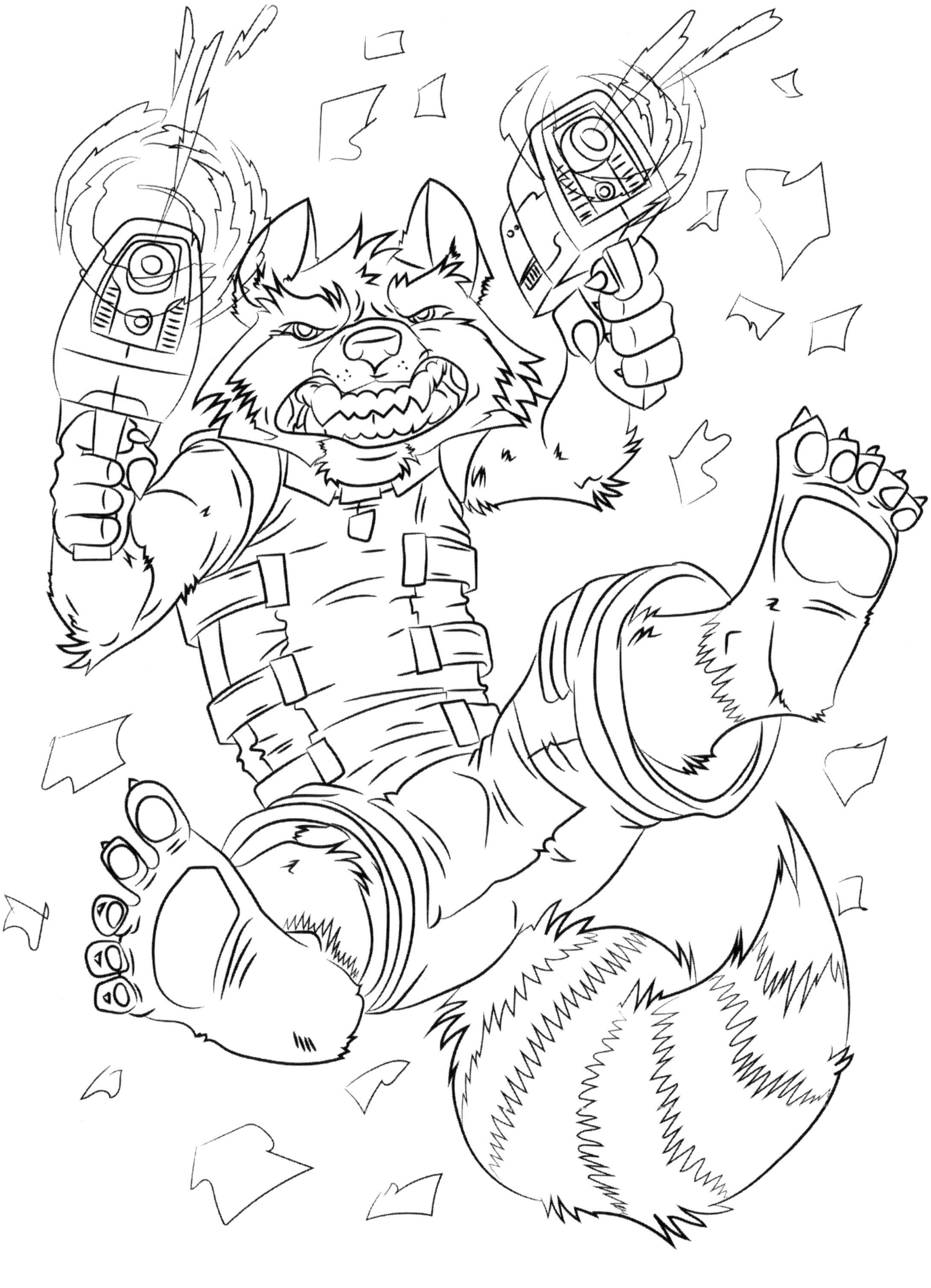

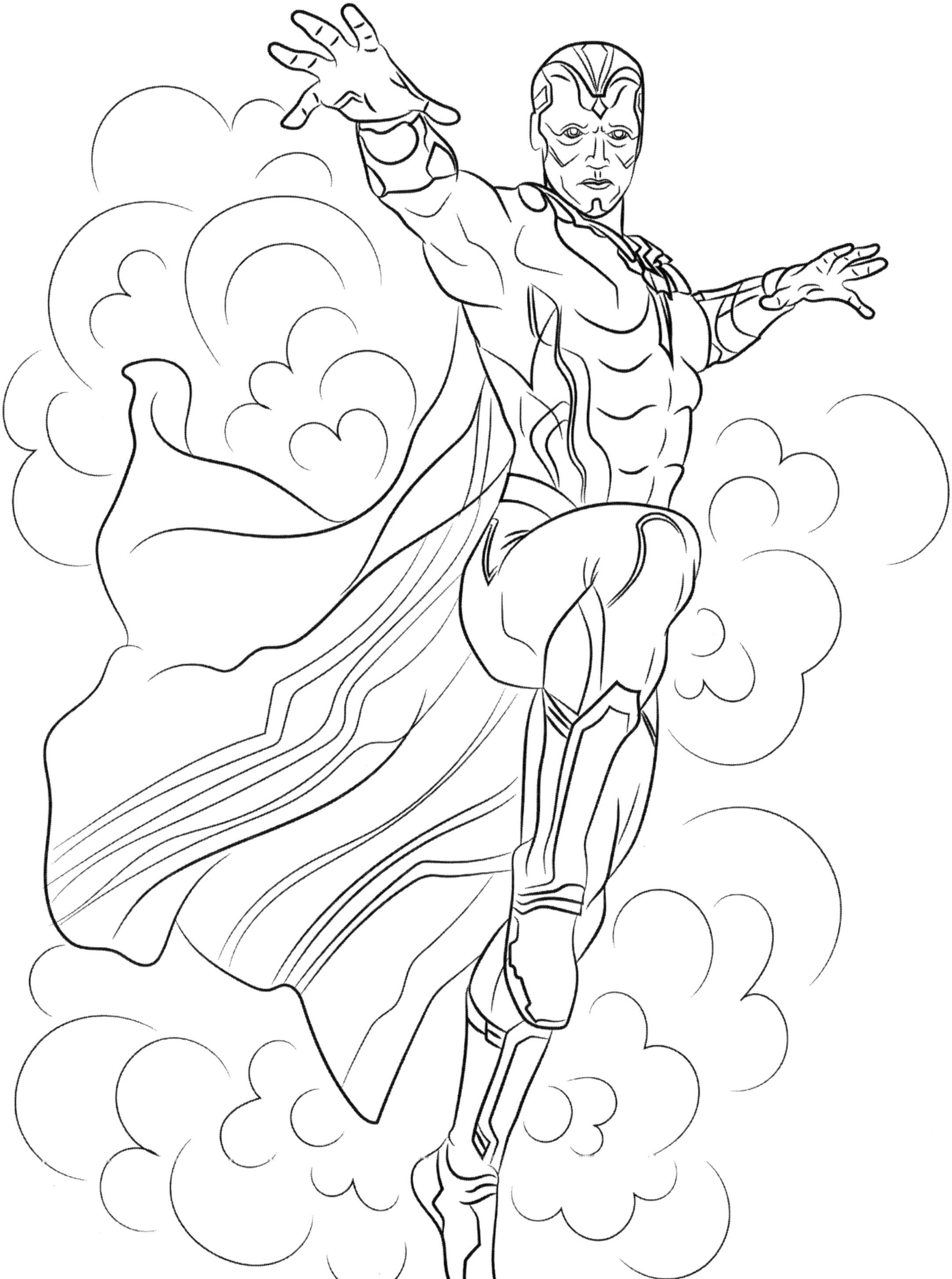

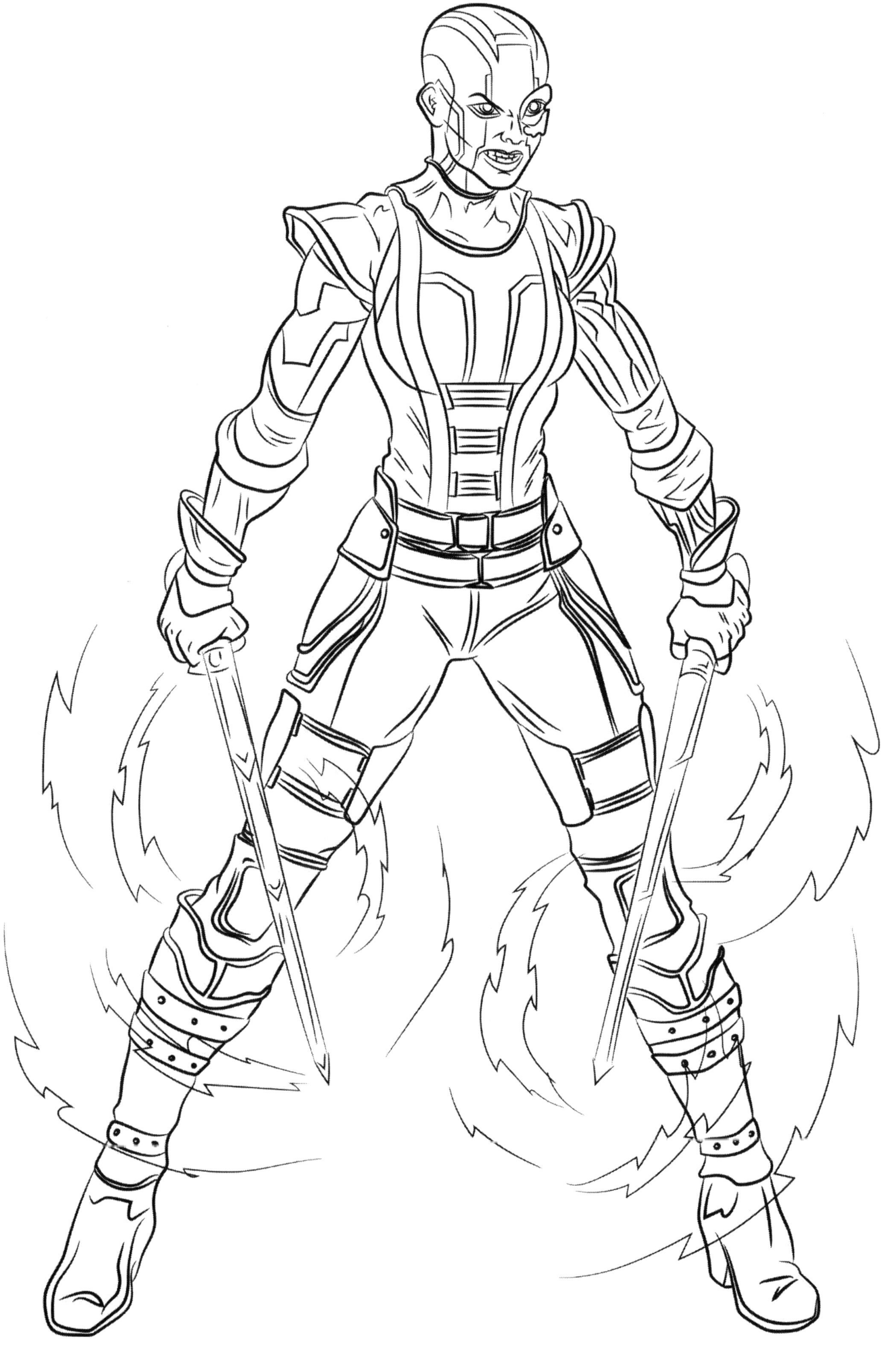

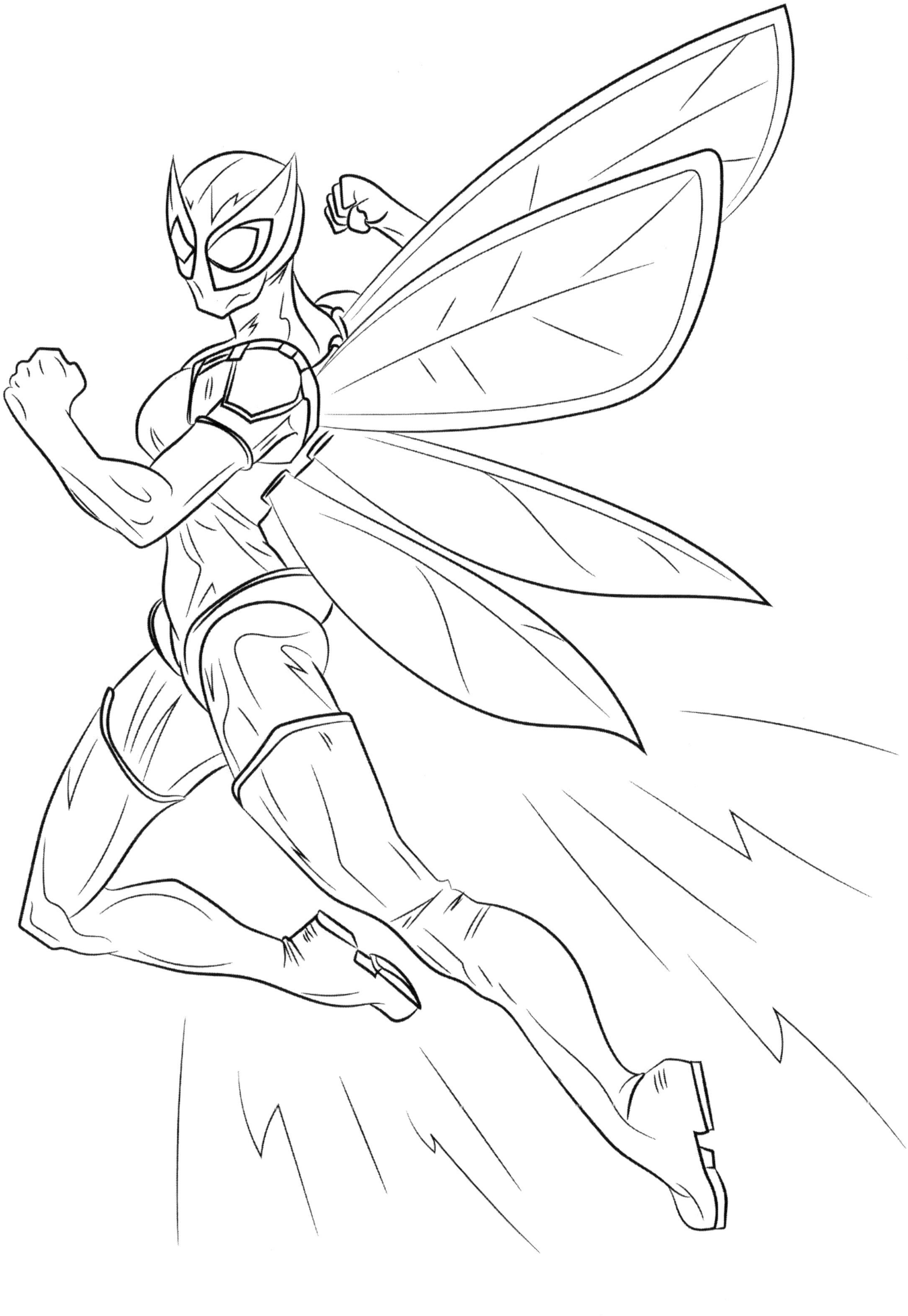

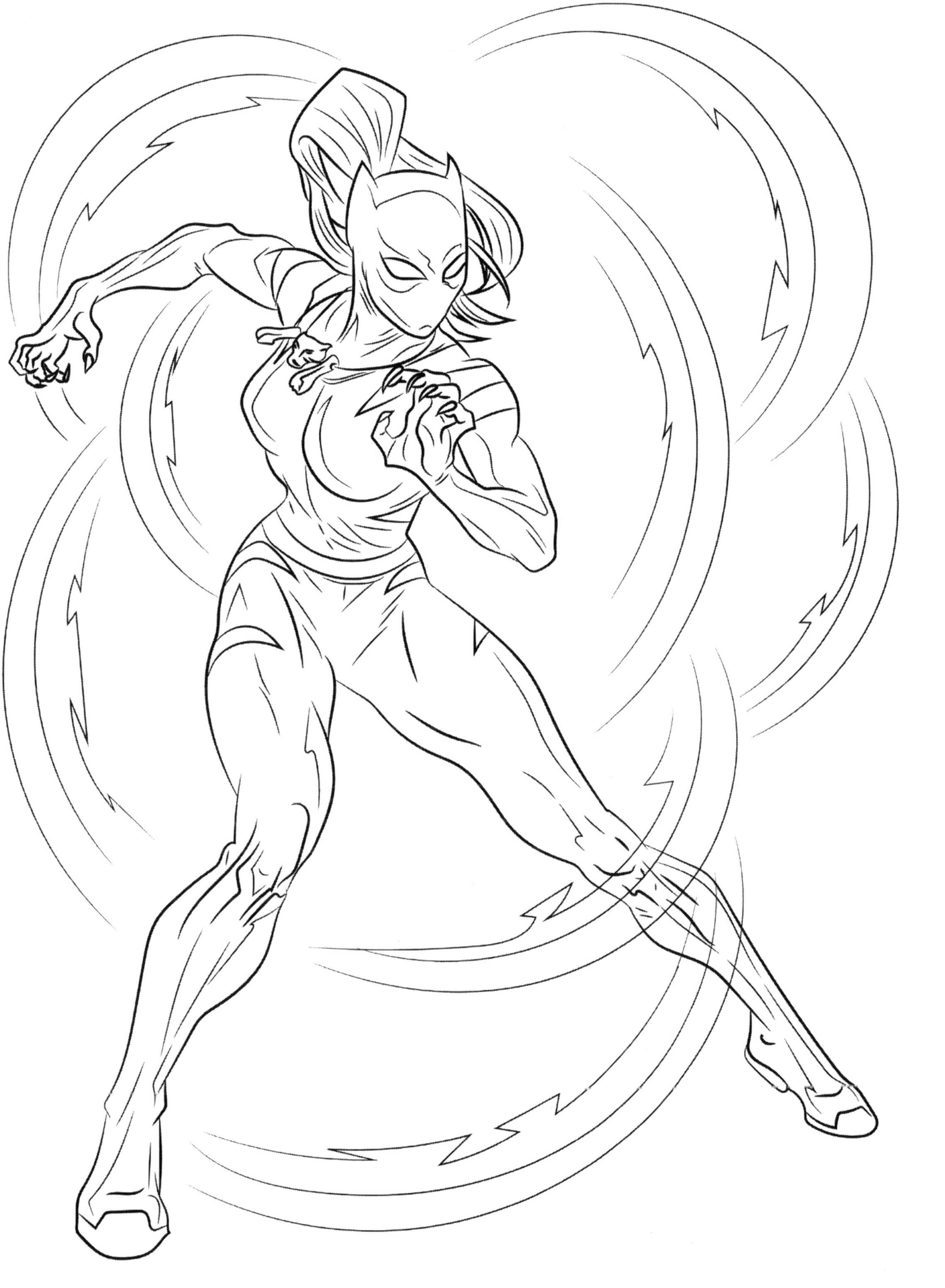

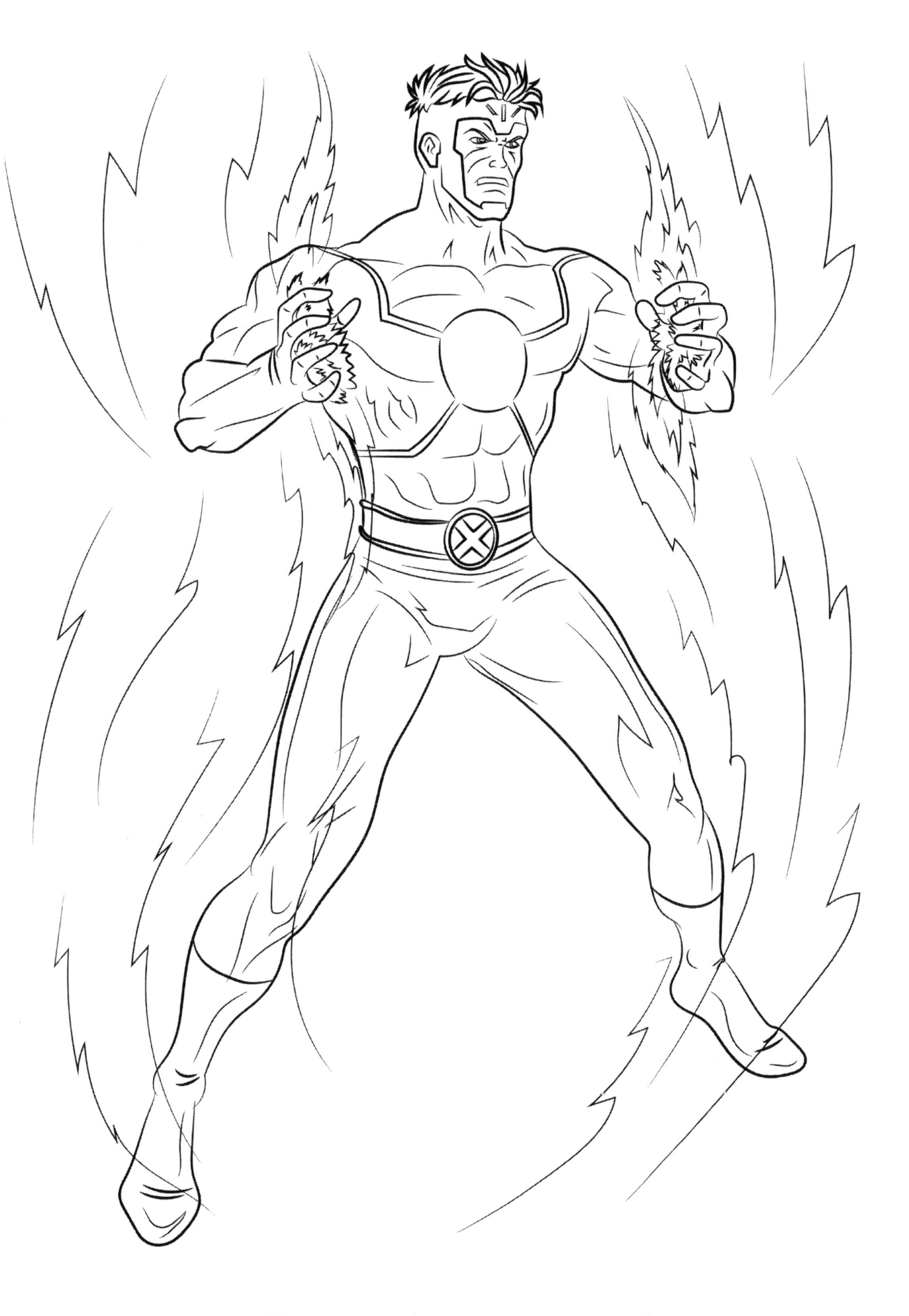

10306453R00038

Made in the USA
San Bernardino, CA
28 November 2018